mini
edition

# The Big Book of Fashion Illustration

D1089129

mini
edition

# The Big Book of Fashion Illustration

## Martin Dawber

BATSFORD

This compact edition first published in the United Kingdom in 2013 by

Batsford
10 Southcombe Street
London W14 0RA

An imprint of Anova Books Company Ltd

Previous edition published 2007

ISBN-13: 9781849941389

A CIP catalogue record for this book is available from the British Library.

10 9 8 7 6 5 4 3 2 1
20 19 18 17 16 15 14 13

Reproduction by Dot Gradations Ltd, UK
Printed by 1010 Printing International Ltd, China

This book can be ordered direct from the publisher at the website: www.anovabooks.com, or try your local bookshop

Distributed in the United States and Canada by Sterling Publishing Co., 387 Park Avenue South, New York, NY 10016, USA

This book is in memory of my father, James Samuel Dawber, and offered with love to my mother, Betty, and my sister, Carole.

'Fashion is not something that exists in dresses only. Fashion is in the sky, in the street; fashion has to do with ideas, the way we live, what is happening'
'Coco' Chanel (1883–1971)

Title page:
Janis Salek
Atelier (2006)
Collage using hand-painted papers

Opposite:
Sonya Suhariyan
Accessories (2006)
Ink/Watercolour/Pen

# Contents

# FOREWORD

Fashion illustration these days is said to be as rare as a snow leopard. To smoke out the images in this exciting book, Martin Dawber has become a kind of Pied Piper eliciting, with a secret digital pitch, the cutting-edge visions of hundreds of snow leopards from all over the world.

Encountering his artists in the light of monitors, at the foot of fashion runways, on the streets of Paris and in the pages of little-known magazines, he found fashion art alive and well – and yet much changed. The artists of today do not just portray fashion in beautiful isolation. They transpose it – with seamless integration – into contemporary lifestyle.

The globalization of all design areas, such as home-style, travel and sports, are revealed in this book. The viewer's identification of these elements, which draws them in with welcome recognition, is made more delightful by the art of the illustrator. Coffee at Starbucks, skateboard ramps, Shoe Fest at Barney's, and even the bedroom, all provide a new stage for the daily interaction of fashion and lifestyle.

This is in front of us everyday, but it is the special terrain of the fashion illustrator to orchestrate and edit the clearest punch. These innovators inspire through their unique expressions – unsurprisingly, they are at the forefront of dictating new trends.

The book's other thread, significant as it ever was, is fashion illustration's most important element – drawing. This is still tantamount, whether the artist is using a Number 4 pencil or a Wacom tablet. Line, like the baton of a skilled maestro, takes the viewer throughout this book. Throughout history, the skilled use of line has earned the credential of being one of the most effective artistic methods used to convey emotion. The confluence of hands-on materials and the latest digital programs results in the increase of fashion illustration being chosen over photography.

The diversity of artwork is also augmented by the fact that these artists come from many cultures and countries. After a while, the reader eagerly attempts to identify the roots of each illustrator and is rather startled to find that East has been busy meeting West.

The fashion illustrator's skill at creating a seductive environmental perfume is joined by an ability to quickly sketch character, to depict emotion and attitude by imposing style. It is here that style from within – or attitude, a major earmark of the fashionistas – ranges from heartbroken women to bored sprawling youth, or angry bad boys flying around the hood like a pack of hornets.

Born of a generation of artists deeply influenced by comic books, music videos and cartoons, the multi-vantage point often enlivens the illustration, inviting the viewers to participate as opposed to keeping them at a distance behind the velvet ropes. For page after page sexuality is brazenly flaunted when needed, creating at times a privileged voyeuristic seat for the viewer, but more often sensuality prevails. This is fashion illustration at its best, incorporating every weapon of seduction. Hang on to your hats and wallets – these formerly endangered artists are out to get you!

Karen Santry, Associate Professor, Fashion Institute of
  Technology, New York
Executive Vice President, Fashion Art Bank Inc. (USA and
  Japan)

# INTRODUCTION

*It's life, Jim, but not as we know it,*
*not as we know it, Captain*
'Star Trekkin'
by The Firm (Lister/John O'Connor)

To paraphrase Mr Spock, fashion illustration has been turned around during the past decade and re-invented for today's more visually conscious audience. Benefiting from its reawakening as the foremost barometer of contemporary lifestyle it remains unique in its ability to articulate fashion.

Berlin-based designer Lulu feels we are experiencing an illustration revolution. '20 years ago, photography was the main media used in fashion magazines. Only a few illustrators worked as commercial artists. It all came back with Wallpaper* magazine – Tyler Brûlé made it possible. He started to use illustration again like magazines had in the 50s'.

Unquestionably, illustration has elbowed itself back into the limelight after only being tolerated in the shadows of photography's monopoly. Indeed, photography's dominance is equally under threat, as current technological advances bring their individual techniques closer together. UK-based illustration duo, Jacqui Paull and Carl Melegari, who combine both photography and illustration in their artwork, prefer the term 'reportage image-makers'. 'We like to fuse the two elements together to achieve our goal. It is more innovative and exciting. We mix a combination of techniques – photography, hand-drawn elements, Xerox, flat graphics – all collaged together using Photoshop to give a more individual approach. We are influenced by fashion and street culture but like to use our observational skills, so to label oneself as purely a 'fashion illustrator' today would not be totally true'.

The ivory-tower exclusivity that cloaked preceding exponents has been replaced with a steady fix of fashion 'in yer face' – shaking off the mothballs of convention in a heady mix of editorial Esperanto and exhibitionism. 'Fashion is more important today than ever' states Australian artist, Vincent Agostino, 'because as the world becomes more populated we will strive to be more individual. Fashion will always give us an identity. We now have the technologies to help us explore the past and future in new ways'. Similarly, Hungarian artist Naomi Devil reveals 'in my work I am interested in how young people find a way of self-expression through the extreme vogues of fashion. Their creativity is an elemental part of my work. The quality of my illustration has changed, because the clothes we have to illustrate have become more eye-catching, more colourful'.

For too long art students were force-fed the misconception that there was an accepted stereotype passing itself off as the elongated, nine-head-length norm. Fashion has never supported the notion of normality – its function is to innovate and revolutionize so why should its graphic representation resist change and stick so closely to an accepted template? Fashion illustration is never solely about the minutiae of garment construction – it is painted in broader brushstrokes and equally concerned with mood, emotion and, above all else, style.

UK university graduate Gemma Waite concurs: 'When you say 'fashion illustration' people always conjure up images of 1940s-style sketches with long, tall legs – fashion illustration is always changing!'. This is a view that Dutch illustrator Irene Jacobs, alias I'm JAC, agrees with: 'In my experience illustration styles change every season, just like fashion or interior and graphic design'.

The once-exclusive club that barred all non-members now flashes an 'All Welcome' sign over the door. The Big Book of Fashion Illustration has flung its net wide, embracing the documentary photo-realism of Yusuke Saitoh (Japan) and Mayrhosby Yeoshen (Venezuela) in contrast to the impressionistic approach of Noumeda Carbone (Italy) and Margot Mace (France). The cleanly articulated pixels of Arthur Mount (USA) and Daniel Chen (Canada) clash with the baroque digital rhythms of Kosmas Apatangelos (Greece) and Ella Tjader (Lithuania). All are adopted along with the tactile fabrications of Borja Uriona (Spain) and Lys Wilcox (USA).

Widening of the doors of participation means newer exponents of fashion illustration are bringing their own personal baggage into the ever-expanding frame, fuelling a visual crossover culture.

California collage artist Christy McCaffrey comments that 'fashion is always going to be important to people. It is the most obvious expression of who you are. How are designers going to explain their vision without a drawing? It remains the most convincing explanation, showing the thought process behind the fashion. A photograph only reflects the end result, the reality'. Of her own distinctive approach, she adds: 'it is important to get the look of the clothing right because it can tell so much about a person. Whether a goth or a jock you have a sort of uniform that explains this. I have always tried to represent that in a believable way'.

During the 20th century, fashion illustrators endured a bumpy ride. Today they are fluent in an unorthodox language that, while encouraging a radical re-think, is fully aware of its rich aesthetic lineage. For Barcelona illustrator Oscar Gimenez, 'fashion has changed a lot. Nowadays it covers a variety of trends. Fashion illustration has evolved from a close-to-reality representation to now capturing the essence of our time in a variety of styles'.

The niche bubble that often pigeon-holed last century's exponents of fashion illustration in their silver-service exclusivity zone, and nearly forced its extinction, has been exploded, exploited and reinvented for this new generation. Claudio Parentela (Italy) subverts the prototype with caricatured illustrations in total contrast to the Art Nouveau outlines from Wai (Japan) – both equally individual and valid treatments of the form.

Now there is an inspirational freedom of expression that challenges each and every illustrator to roll the dice and, by rising to the challenge, push their work to the limit. Tokyo-born illustrator Yuko Shimizu affirms from his New York studio, that the 'possibilities are limitless. The only limit is that of our imagination and creativity'. A view supported by Russian artist Sonya Suhariyan; 'It is now possible to draw everything – illustration gives free rein to your imagination'.

Formal recognition has improved with wide-reaching exhibitions acknowledging their output alongside that of more mainstream artists. As part of the Amsterdam International Fashion Week 2006, 48 illustrators were presented in How Do You Do? Deconstructing Illustration. Across the world at the Alliance Francaise in Bangalore, there was Traits Très Mode, an exhibition featuring contemporary French fashion illustration. Solo retrospectives are on the increase. London played host to the dramatic illustrations of David Downton (Couture Voyeur) while in Hamburg, the pop-inspired graphic illustrator Jasper Goodall, blazed in his own five-year retrospective (God of Illustration).

As 'fast fashion' became the drip feed for today's consumer fashion victim, technological advances have given illustrators access to a fashion awareness that speaks a different language from two decades ago. 'Catwalks' are no longer restricted to salons in Paris and Milan – video streaming the latest pop icon can have more direct impact on contemporary style.

Australian fashion designer and illustrator John Prikryl admits that historically 'illustrating within the fashion industry was generic across the board. Technological advances have changed the meaning of the term 'fashion illustration'. Technology has opened doors to entirely new worlds of illustration that allows each creator more freedom in media, methods, and so on. The difference is that almost anything can be considered 'fashion illustration' these days'.

In The Big Book of Fashion Illustration, illustrators are fully in tune with this new frequency and articulate their reactions in directions that are exciting and innovative. While some remain exponents of traditional media, others epitomise the PlayStation generation that encountered digital technology at their mother's knee. 'The arrival of computers has had a massive impact', acknowledges UK artist Claire Baker. 'It has allowed illustration to evolve', while Korean illustrator Woonyoung Chang adds that although computers can 'make everything easier, you still have to know how to use your hand. The computer is only a tool like your pen or brush'.

Streetwise Filipino illustrator Jason Jaring maintains 'technology affects everything – commerce, politics, art. Fashion illustrators always want to try out new media. There are things you can do with digital media that you can't do with traditional illustration, but ultimately, software programs are just another medium – they have limits. What is limitless is each artist's own creativity and imagination. The product is more important than the process. If you do it with computer software – great. If you can do it with a pen and paper – cool'.

Increasingly there are illustrators operating like scratch DJs, mixing and sampling everything that comes within their skill arena, whether it be time-honored analog or new-age digital. Boundaries continue to be blurred. Gimenez also acknowledges that 'previously, an illustrator was somebody who could draw. Nowadays many other artists, with skills ranging from photography to graffiti, can produce amazing illustrations. It has broadened the number of resources for the rest of us'.

Be it the spontaneous gesture of graphite hitting paper or a virtual layering of pixels, the challenge is to stretch the envelope in ever-increasing personal and individual reworkings. Their work continues to register as an allegory of contemporary lifestyle.

The Big Book of Fashion Illustration is laid out like a worldwide directory of style, championing a unique assembly of over 250 international artists and illustrators whose loyalties and experience lie within fashion, but no longer feel happy with their 'fashion illustrator' label. They deem it is too limiting a nomenclature – looking over their shoulders rather than to the future. Is the term 'fashion illustration' now passed its own sell-by date? – most prefer to shelter in the inclusive umbrella of 'fashion artist'.

Whatever their eventual classification, I owe a huge debt of gratitude to these featured artists, who were so gracious with their time and generous with their artwork – this book stands testament to their outstanding talent.

Martin Dawber

Arturo Elena
Untitled, for
*Cosmopolitan,*
Spain (2004)
Ink/Felt tip pen

# Womenswear

separates   knit   coats & jackets

eveningwear   couture   bridal   lingerie

Bil Donovan
MAG (2006)
Ink/Gouache

Hayato Jome
A Small Bag (2003)
Acrylic on paper

Laura Laine
Girl with Blouse (2005)
Pencil/Marker pen

Laura Laine
Untitled (2006)
Pencil

Claire Anderson
Fleur (2005)
Stitched cotton thread on calico

Arthur Mount
Striped Shirt (2001)
Adobe Illustrator

Ella Tjader
Patterns Craze (2005)
Adobe Illustrator/Adobe Photoshop

Pascale Evrard
Easter Girl (2006)
Ink/Watercolour/Pencil/Adobe Photoshop

Michael Sibley
Kim (2002)
Oils, glass and gold on plywood

Claire Anderson
Anna and Annabelle (2005)
Stitched cotton thread on calico

Lys Wilcox
Kimora (2004)
Collage/Cut paper

Lys Wilcox
Carol Ann (2004)
Collage/Cut paper

Jonas Bergstrand
Neiman Marcus Womenswear, New York (2005)
Adobe Illustrator/Adobe Photoshop

Nicoletta Mazzesi
Rising (2006)
Adobe Photoshop/Adobe Illustrator

Cecilia Carlstedt
Nordiska Kompaniet
(2006)
Pencil/Ink/Adobe
Illustrator/
Adobe Photoshop

Samantha Wilson
London Shopping (2006)

Lopetz:BD
Lu Blick (2002)
Adobe Photoshop

Carlo Stanga
Celine (2004)
Adobe Photoshop

Emily Peach
Untitled (2004)

Pinglet
Mini (2002)
Adobe Illustrator

Bil Donovan
MAG Spring (2005)
Ink/Gouache

Alex Green
Bernice (2006)
Pencil/Paint/Pen/
Collage/Adobe Photoshop

Anna Cangialosi
Waiting (2005)
Acrylic and tissue on wood

Kim Rosen
Earthy Student (2004)
Ink/Acrylic/Adobe Photoshop

Erica Sharp
Floral Print (2005)
Adobe Photoshop/Adobe Illustrator

Tatsuro Kuichi
Untitled (2002)
Adobe Photoshop

Stina Persson
Alviero Martini Dress (2004)
Ink/Coloured pencil

Yuko Yoshioka
Etude (2006)
Adobe Photoshop

Rainer Stolle
Untitled (2005)
Pencil/Watercolour/Ad
obe Photoshop

Rainer Stolle
Untitled (2005)
Pencil/Watercolour/Adobe Photoshop

LiXian Teng
Aunt Judy (2006)
Adobe Photoshop/Adobe Illustrator

Valeria Docampo
Sir JM Barrie Style (2005)
Adobe Illustrator

Menisha
Let's Drive! (2005)
Adobe Photoshop

Rainer Stolle
Pressure-sensitive Skin (2006)
Pressure-sensitive tape/Rubber/Pencil/Adobe Photoshop

Irene Jacobs
Starsign Cancer (2004)
Adobe Illustrator

Astrid Mueller (Potatomammadesign)
Untitled (2006)
Corel Painter/Adobe Illustrator

Edel Rodriguez
My Father's Sweater (2005)
Pastel and ink on paper

Tatsuro Kuichi
Untitled (2006)

Raissa Gabriel
Scheme Walk (2005)
Ink/Marker pen

Christian Barthold
Summer Wind (2005)
India ink/Adobe Photoshop/Adobe Illustrator

Bella Pilar
Turtles (2005)
Gouache

Malena Gagliesi
Fussy Knitting, Vogue Knitting, NYC (2003)
Adobe Illustrator

Anna Cangialosi
Portlandia (2006)
Acrylic and tissue on wood

Arturo Elena
Untitled, for *Mujer Hoy* (2005)
Ink/Felt tip pen

Jenny Williamson
Untitled (2006)
Pencil/Watercolour/Adobe Photoshop

Nicoletta Mazzesi
AVX (2005)
Ink/Adobe Photoshop

Sam Wilson
Eye Candy (2004)
Pen/Ink/Adobe Photoshop

Raissa Gabriel
Chilled (2004)
Oil pastels

Claire Anderson
Grace and Churchill (2005)
Stitched cotton thread on calico

Eva Byrne
Aruba Fall Collection (2005)
Adobe Photoshop

Lopetz:BD
Parisanne (2002)
Digital camera/Adobe Photoshop

Lulu
Untitled (2003)
Adobe Photoshop/Adobe Illustrator

David Knight
Anna in Kente Double Coat by Vusi (2006)
Corel Draw

Annie Boberg
Autumn (2000)
Corel Painter/
Adobe Photoshop

Anna Kiper
Model in Tweed (2006)
Marker/Coloured pencil

Tatsuro Kuichi
Untitled (2004)
Adobe Photoshop

Cecilia Carlstedt
Untitled (2004)
Pencil/Adobe Illustrator

Yuko Shimizu
Untitled, for *The Village Voice* (2003)
Ink/Adobe Photoshop

Gavin Reece
Mrs Mills (2005)
Adobe Photoshop

Fhiona Galloway
Salvatore (2006)
Macromedia FreeHand

Andrea Byrne
Cordelia's Corsage (2004)
Watercolour/Ink on paper

Natascha Engelmann
Stroke (2003)
Pencil/Adobe Illustrator

Alessandra Scandella
Lady with Brooch (2005)
Corel Painter/Adobe Photoshop

41

Terence Lawlor
Yamamoto, Fall 2006 (2006)
Collage

Kerstin Wacker
Forest (2006)
Pen/Watercolour/Adobe Photoshop

Prot Srimekhanond
Untitled (2004)
Adobe Photoshop

Michael Sibley
Emma (2002)
Oils, acrylic and fabric on canvas

Andrea Byrne
Trinity (2003)
Watercolour/Ink on paper

Alessandra Scandella
Black Lady (2005)
Corel Painter/Adobe
Photoshop

45

Michael Sibley
Jo (2004)
Oils, glass and gold on plywood

Genevieve Kelly
Morning Sunrise (2005)
Pencil/Collage/Photograph/Adobe Photoshop

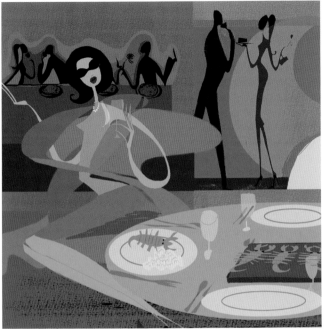

Alessandra Scandella
San Pellegrino (2005)
Corel Painter/Adobe Photoshop

Valeria Docampo
The Taste of Cherries (2005)
Adobe Illustrator

47

Terence Lawlor
Body Chic (1995)
Collage

Amparo Losana
Louis de Gama for *Daily ModaLisboa* magazine (2004)
Soft Pastels

Bil Donovan
Lounge Girls (2005)
Ink/Gouache

Arturo Elena
Untitled, for Reina Sofia Museum, Madrid (2003)
Ink/Felt tip pen

Cybèle
Goddess Five
(2003)
Adobe
Illustrator

Cybèle
Goddess One
(2003)
Adobe
Illustrator

Cybèle
Goddess Four
(2003)
Adobe
Illustrator

Cybèle
Goddess Two
(2003)
Adobe
Illustrator

Karen Santry
Bumble Bee
Girl Walking
Pugs (2006)
Oil on wood
cutouts/Wire

Manna Lai
Butterfly (2005)
Pencil/Adobe Photoshop

Lopetz:BD
Pink Dress (1994)
Pencil/Crayon

Manna Lai
Christmas (2005)
Pencil/Adobe Photoshop

Ariel Mazo
Untitled (2005)
Ink/Gouache

Serena Waldron
Serenity (2005)
Adobe Photoshop

Bella Pilar
Snowflake Gown (2004)
Gouache

Alexander Brooke Smith
Hera (2006)
Mixed-media collage/Watercolour

Arturo Elena
Untitled, for Reina Sofia Museum, Madrid (2003)
Ink/Felt tip pen

Bil Donovan
Glam Girl (2004)
Ink

Stina Persson
"Oops!", Versace (2004)
Ink/Watercolour dyes/Adobe Photoshop

Ariel Mazo
Untitled (2005)
Ink/Pastel

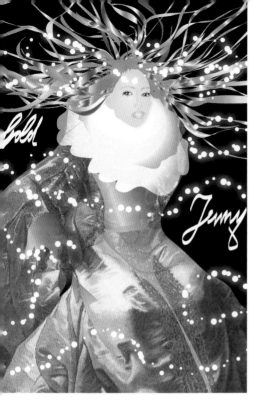

Natascha Engelmann
Goldjenny (2002)
Collage/Adobe Photoshop/Adobe Illustrator

Sonya Suhariyan
Autumn (2005)
Gouache/Acrylic/Felt pen

Claire Ann Baker
Edith (2003)
Collage/Gouache/Machine embroidery

Valeria Docampo
Milky Way Dress (2005)
Adobe Illustrator

Bil Donovan
Setarium Couture (1999)
Graphite pastel/Gouache

Claire Ann Baker
Tallulah (2003)
Magazine collage/Embellishment

Anna Kiper
Evening Outfit (2000)
Watercolour

Annie Boberg
Lady in Pink (2000)
Corel Painter/Adobe Photoshop

Margot Mace van Huijkelom
Dance (2006)
Watercolour/Ink pen

Janis Salek
Wedding Belle (2005)
Watercolour

Marsha Silvestri
Portrait of a Bride with Roses (2004)
Pencil/Pastel/Adobe Photoshop

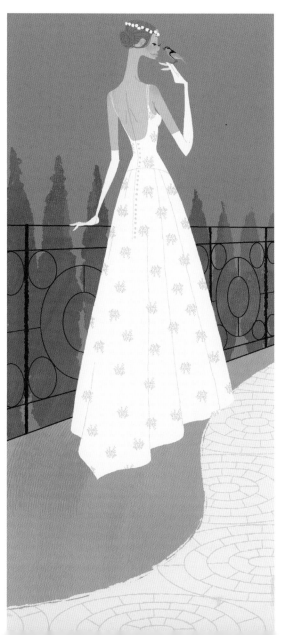

Yuko Yoshioka
Robe de Mariage (2005)
Adobe Photoshop

Bil Donovan
Estée Lauder Shopping
Bag (1996)
Watercolour

Gillian Cook
Wedding Day (2005)
Adobe Photoshop

Karen Santry
Gangsta Rapper's Daughter Bride (2006)
Oil on rosewood

Jennie Yip
Spring Bride (2006)
Gouache on paper

Nina Edwards
Young Bride and Her Sisters (2006)
Adobe Illustrator/Adobe Photoshop

Christophe Lardot
La Panne (2006)
Adobe Photoshop

Wai
Lingerie
(2004)
Adobe
Illustrator/
Adobe
Photoshop

Yuko Yoshioka
Salles de Repos
(2006)
Adobe
Photoshop

Amparo Losana
D&G (2006)
Adobe Photoshop

Annabelle J. Verhoye
Vanity Fair (2006)
Chine collé/Adobe Photoshop

Menisha
Pink Room (2005)
Adobe Photoshop

Meirav Shaul
A Girl with a Tiger (2004)
Acrylic on paper

Lopetz:BD
Sonneblume (2002)
Adobe Photoshop

Sally Pring
Untitled (2006)
Pencil/Adobe Photoshop

Chico Hayasaki
Good Morning (2002)
Adobe Photoshop

Erica Sharp
Androgyne
(2005)
Adobe
Photoshop/
Adobe
Illustrator

Fhiona Galloway
Sparkle (2005)
Macromedia FreeHand

J. David McKenney
Peepshow (2005)
Ink/Adobe Photoshop

Arturo Elena
Untitled, for Custo Barcelona (2005)
Ink/Felt tip pen

Kim Longhurst
Dream Girl (1998)
Macromedia FreeHand/Adobe Photoshop

Laura Niles
Subtract Lingerie (2005)
Pencil/Adobe Photoshop

Nicoletta Mazzesi
Dancing Threads (2005)
Ink/Adobe Photoshop/Adobe Illustrator

Borja Uriarte
Lady Chair (2005)
Fabric

Bil Donovan
Lingerie Pin Up (1998)
Graphite pastel

Lucy Allen
Private Commission, Untitled
(2005)
Ink pen/Adobe Photoshop

Bella Pilar
Pink Art (2005)
Gouache

Marsha Silvestri
Michelle in Mermaid Pose (2003)
Charcoal/Adobe Photoshop/Adobe
Illustrator

73

# Menswear

tees&shirts  outerwear  knit  casual

neckwear  smart  bespoke  underwear

Margot Mace van Huijkelom
Romeo (2006)
Watercolour/Ink pen

James Holman
Disco Micheal (2006)
Graphite/Ink/Pencil/Crayon/Felt tip

Pinglet
Dragon (2002)
Adobe Illustrator

Hellovon
Owl (2005)
Pencil/Photogra
phy/Ink/Adobe
Illustrator

Marguerite Sauvage
Styling Research (2005)
Ink/Adobe Photoshop

Cesar de la Rosa
Miami Summer (2004)
Adobe Illustrator

Michael Crampton
Bar Talk (2005)
Adobe Photoshop

Alessandra Scandella
A Man (2005)
Corel Painter/
Adobe Photoshop

Lopetz:BD
Tom (2002)
Adobe Photoshop

Wahid Ahmadyar
Shirt (2006)
Pencil/Watercolour

Dorothea Renault
3 Men Arriving (2005)
Adobe Illustrator

Lee Woodgate
The Big Chill (2002)
Adobe Photoshop

Meirav Shaul
Alon (2004)
Acrylic on paper

Monica Laita
NY Estate Agency N.1 (2006)
Adobe Photoshop

Irene Jacobs
Untitled, for 'A Man's Guide to Life',
Man magazine (1999)
Adobe Photoshop/Adobe Illustrator

Naomi Austin
Neon City (2006)
Adobe Illustrator/
Adobe Photoshop

Kim Rosen
Sporty Student (2004)
Ink/Acrylic/Adobe
Photoshop

Jacqui Paull and Carl Melegari
Joey (2006)
Adobe Photoshop

Kun-Sung Chung
Three Guys (2004)
Adobe Illustrator

Paul Watmough
We Know (2006)
Pen/Ink/Adobe Photoshop

Irene Jacobs
Indulgence 1, for Philips Design (2002)
Adobe Illustrator

Arthur Mount
Jil Sander (2003)
Adobe Illustrator

Harmind Singh Arora
Red Happiness (2004)
Coloured pencil

Arthur Mount
Kojima (2003)
Adobe Illustrator

Elena Lavdovskaya Konstantinovna
TSUM Menswear Campaign (2005)
Aquarelle/Ink/Adobe Photoshop

Yolanda Gonzalez
Jeans (2006)
Gouache on paper

Harmind Singh Arora
Denim Feel (2003)
Coloured pencil

Marsha Silvestri
Crayon Denim Man (1984)
Coloured pencil/Crayon/
Adobe Photoshop

Jamal 'Bam' Tate
Untitled (2002)
Pen/Ink/Adobe Illustrator

Wahid Ahmadyar
Bomber (2006)
Pencil/Watercolour

Rachel Messenger
Untitled (2006)
Ink/Pencil/Adobe Photoshop

Maximilian Doerr
Untitled (2005)
Collage

Emily Peach
Big Coat
(2004)
Collage/Paint/
Chalk

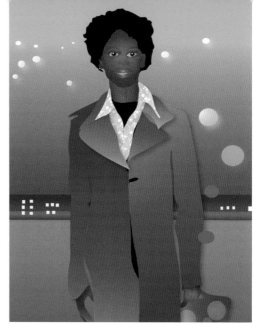

Natascha
Engelmann
Ghettoblaster
(2000)
Pencil/Adobe
Photoshop

Koichiro
Furukawa
Shadow on
the Wall
(2006)
Pencil/Sten
cil/Adobe
Photoshop

Sonya Suhariyan
Marginal Man (2005)
Ink/Watercolour/Pen

Maximilian Doerr
Untitled (2004)
Collage

Mayrhosby Yeoshen
The Bishounen (2004)
Adobe Photoshop/Corel Painter

Chico Hayasaki
T-shirt (2003)
Adobe Photoshop

Marsha Silvestri
Man in Hat and Sweater (1984)
Crayola Crayon

Javier Joaquin
Airbourne Clothes (2004)
Adobe Illustrator

Elena Lavdovskaya Konstantinovna
Tsum Menswear Campaign (2005)
Aquarelle/Ink/Adobe Photoshop

Bil Donovan
EV Hipster (2000)
Ink/Pastel/Gouache/Graphite

Marsha Silvestri
Zipper Jacket (2003)
Charcoal/Adobe Illustrator

Lee Woodgate
Fred Perry (2003)
Adobe Photoshop

Lior Yefet Tabib
Beard Guy (Self Portrait) (2005)
Adobe Photoshop

Christian
Barthold
Endless
Summer
(2000)
India
ink/Gouache/
Adobe
Photoshop

Irene Jacobs
Indulgence 2,
for Philips
Design (2002)
Adobe
Illustrator

Arthur Mount
Marc Jacobs
(2003)
Adobe
Illustrator

Tatsuro Kuichi
Untitled (2005)
Adobe
Photoshop

Irene Jacobs
Summer Trends, for Esquire
magazine (2003)
Adobe Illustrator

Pascale Evrard
Autumn Boy (2006)
Ink/Watercolour/Pencil/Adobe Photoshop

Marsha Silvestri
Brown Zip Jacket (2004)
Charcoal/Adobe Photoshop/Adobe Illustrator

Monica Laita
NY Estate Agency N.2 (2006)
Adobe Photoshop

Bil Donovan
Geoffry Beene (2004)
Ink

Mariko Yamazaki
Reading Man on Chair with Book (2003)
Adobe Illustrator

Jacqui Paull
and Carl
Melegari
Aadel and
Rokit (2003)
Adobe
Photoshop

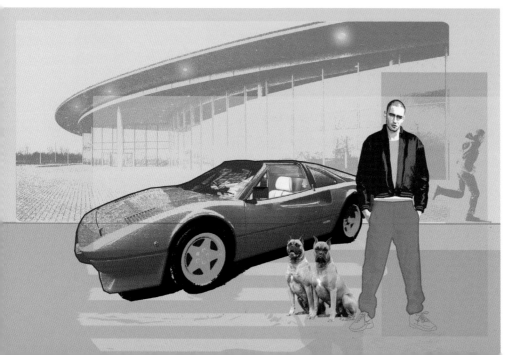

Jacqui Paull and
Carl Melegari
Guy's Car (2002)
Adobe Photoshop

Mariko Yamazaki
The Man Who Turns His Back (2003)
Adobe Illustrator

Jacquie O'Neill
Cool Guys Wear Pink! (2005)
Adobe Illustrator

Anton Storey
Raymond (2002)
Pen/Adobe Illustrator

Bil Donovan
Pitti L'uomo (2001)
Ink/Pastel on BFK paper

Elena Lavdovskaya Konstantinovna
TSUM Menswear Campaign (2005)
Aquarelle/Ink/Adobe Photoshop

Michinori Naro
A Man (2004)
Chinese ink/Coloured ink/Pencil

Bil Donovan
Untitled (2000)
Conté/Pastel/Gouache

Janis Salek
Parisian Dandy (2006)
Adobe Photoshop

Bil Donovan
Unititled (1999)
Pastel/Gouache

Margot Mace van Huijkelom
An English Man (2006)
Watercolour/Ink pen

Jennie Yip
Excello Shirts (2006)
Gouache on watercolour paper

Lee Woodgate
Electric Six (2005)
Adobe Photoshop

John Prikryl
85 Sylvan (2005)
Sketchpad/Adobe Photoshop/
Adobe Illustrator

John Prikryl
Studio Z1 (2005)
Sketchpad/Adobe
Photoshop/
Adobe Illustrator

Laura Laine
Daniel (2005)
Pencil

Margot Mace van Huijkelom
Jamel (2006)
Watercolour/Ink pen

Tina Berning
Männermode (2004)
Felt pen/Watercolour/Vector
Graphic/Adobe Photoshop

Tina Berning
Männermode (2004)
Felt pen/Watercolour/Vector
Graphic/Adobe Photoshop

Elena Lavdovskaya Konstantinovna
TSUM Menswear Campaign (2005)
Aquarelle/Ink/Adobe Photoshop

Shiho Matsubara
Man with Flowers (2006)
Adobe Illustrator

Pascale Evrard
Man in Blue Jacket (2006)
Ink/Watercolour/Pencil/Adobe Photoshop

Jonas Bergstrand
Neiman Marcus Menswear, New York (2005)
Adobe Illustrator/Adobe Photoshop

Valeria Docampo
Premium Room (2005)
Adobe Illustrator

Jonas Bergstrand
Neiman Marcus Menswear, New York (2005)
Adobe Illustrator/Adobe Photoshop

Gavin Reece
Metro Sexual (2003)
Adobe Photoshop

Yoco Nagamiya
Untitled (2006)
Ink

Wai
Dapper (2005)
Adobe Illustrator/
Adobe Photoshop

Herman Yap
Cool Dude for Nivea
Men (2005)
Macromedia
FreeHand/Adobe
Photoshop

Margot Mace van
Huijkelom
Two Guys (2006)
Watercolour/Ink pen

Pinglet
Styleguy (2002)
Adobe Illustrator

Coburn
Man in White
(2006)
Adobe
Illustrator

Anton Storey
Untitled (2001)
Pen/Adobe Illustrator

Ulis Darama
It's Me! (2005)
Macromedia
FreeHand

Anton Storey
Bob (2003)
Pen/Adobe Illustrator

Taryn Lee
Ryan Gosling (2005)
Adobe Illustrator

Natascha
Engelmann
Brotherhood
(2004)
Pencil/Adobe
Photoshop

Fhiona
Galloway
Nick Cave
(2006)
Macromedia
FreeHand

Irene Jacobs
Summer
Trends, for
*Esquire*
magazine
(2003)
Adobe
Illustrator

Jennie Yip
Salamandra (2006)
Pencil on paper

Terence Lawlor
The b Brothers (1994)
Collage

Andrew Smith
Break Down (2006)
Adobe Photoshop

Aitor Throup
Still Life #28 (2005)
Pencil/watercolour

Kaja Jamtli
Reformed White Suit for Andrew Ibi (2006)
Pencil/Pen/Adobe Photoshop/Adobe Illustrator

Gavin Reece
Style Snob (2004)
Adobe Photoshop

Robert Weiss
The Metrosexual (2004)
Adobe Illustrator

Alessandra Scandella
A Man in Black (2005)
Corel Painter/Adobe Photoshop

Anton Storey
Erik (2004)
Pen/Adobe Photoshop

Yoco Nagamiya
Untitled (2006)
Ink

Arturo Elena
Untitled, for Biendi shop window (2001)
Ink/Felt tip pen

Vincent Agostino
Gucci Summer (2004)
Acrylic/Fabric

Dilek Peker
Perfect Day (2006)
Adobe Photoshop

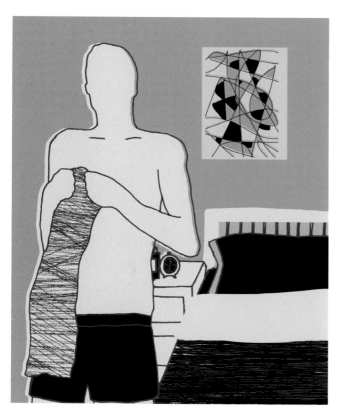

Tiffany Lynch
Bedroom Boy (2006)
Pen/Ink/Adobe Photoshop

Pascale Evrard
Guy in Underwear (2006)
Ink/Watercolour/Pencil/Adobe Photoshop

Nick Larrett
James, Sitting (2005)
Adobe Photoshop

Daniel Mackie
Respect (2003)
Pen/Ink/Adobe Photoshop

Stuart Holmes
Marks and Spencer, basic range (2003)
Adobe Illustrator

# Youth Culture

music  clubland  tribes&vibes

streetfashiongirls  streetwiseguys  relationships

Anton Storey
Untitled (2002)
Pen/Adobe
Illustrator

Irene Jacobs
Untitled, for 'A
Man's Guide
to Life', *Man*
magazine
(1999)
Adobe
Illustrator

Zed
DJ, *DJ World* Magazine (2002)
Adobe Illustrator

Masa
Ghetto Blaster (2005)
Coloured marker pen

David Nwokedi
Ray (2004)
Pencil/Adobe Photoshop

Christian Barthold
Free Your Mind (2006)
India ink/Adobe Photoshop

Jacquie O'Neill
Lost in Music (2005)
Adobe Illustrator CS

Christopher King
Guitar Girl (2005)
Pen/Ink/Adobe Photoshop

Yuko Yoshioka
Guitare (2006)
Adobe Photoshop

Ewa Brockway
Party Girls
(2005)
Adobe
Photoshop

Marguerite Sauvage
Ukulele Orchestra (2005)
Pencil/Adobe Photoshop

Nicoletta Mazzesi
New Scene (2005)
Adobe Photoshop/Adobe Illustrator

John Jay Cabuay
The Jealous Guy
Pen/Ink/Adobe Photoshop

Erica Glasier
Butterfly (2002)
Adobe
Photoshop/Adobe
Illustrator

Rian Hughes
Automatic Anthems (1998)

Marcella Peluffo
Beach Party (2005)

Jeff Mulawka
Clubland (2004)
Adobe Photoshop

Sofia Dias
Pink Neon Dream (2004)
Macromedia FreeHand

Annabelle J Verhoye
La Samaritaine (2006)
Chine collé/Adobe Photoshop

Naomi Devil
Punk (2005)
Oil on canvas

Stuart Mason
Jane (2004)
Oil/Acrylic

Sarah Turner
Punk Rocker
Listening
to Music
(2006)
Adobe
Illustrator

Stuart Holmes
'Punks', for the V&A Museum (2004)
Adobe Illustrator

Erica Glasier
Found (2002)
Adobe Illustrator

Claudio Parentela
Untitled (2005)
Ink and pen on paper

Ewa Brockway
Tyra (2005)
Adobe Photoshop

Gavin Reece
Brazilian! (2004)
Adobe Photoshop

Aga Baranska
Blondie (2006)
Collage/Paint/
Adobe
Photoshop

Giulio Iurissevich
UFO Dictactor (2006)
Macromedia
FreeHand/Adobe
Photoshop

Paul Austin
Volcano Girls (2006)
Pencil/Watercolour

Cecilia Carlstedt
Untitled, *Habit* Magazine (2005)
Pencil/Adobe Illustrator/Adobe Photoshop

Jan Feindt
Personal (2005)
Pen/Ink/Adobe Photoshop

Bella Pilar
Snakes and Butterflies (2005)
Gouache

Bella Pilar
Good Luck Tat (2004)
Gouache

Mayrhosby Yeoshen
Yaoi Boy (2006)
Adobe Photoshop/Corel Painter

Paul Watmough
We Know (2006)
Pen/Ink/Adobe Photoshop

Joseph S Arruda
Kyraa (2003)
Adobe Photoshop/GNU Image
Manipulation Program

Joseph S Arruda
Kyraa (2003)
Adobe Photoshop/GNU Image
Manipulation Program

Naomi Devil
Hip-Hop Girl
(2006)
Oil on canvas

Amparo Losana
Untitled (2005)
Adobe Photoshop

Christopher King
Last Summer (2006)
Pen/Ink/Adobe Photoshop

Gemma Waite
Ghetto Blaster (2005)
Felt pen/Biro/Graphite

Christopher King
Tattoo (2005)
Pen/Ink/Adobe Photoshop

Jeeyun Lee
bf4ever (2005)
Watercolour

Gemma Waite
One World (2006)
Felt pen/Biro/Graphite/
Collage/Adobe Photoshop

Helen Turner
Rollercoaster (2003)
Ink/Adobe Photoshop

Kun-Sung Chung
Fashion Swap & Show, *Let's Party!*, Lobster Press (2004)
Adobe Illustrator

Susie Tsan-Ching Yang
Surfer Girl in Crochet Sweater (2004)
Adobe Illustrator

Giulio Iurissevich
Metropoli (2005)
Macromedia FreeHand/Adobe Illustrator

Varshesh Joshi
Untitled (2004)
Pencil/Ink/Macromedia FreeHand/
Adobe Flash/Adobe Photoshop

Stuart Holmes
Fashion Victim, *Computer Arts* (2004)
Adobe Illustrator

Anna Cangialosi
Louise Clements (2006)
Acrylic and tissue on wood

Laura Laine
Girl with Glasses (2006)
Pencil

Erica Sharp
Tokyo Tomboy (2005)
Adobe Photoshop

151

Laura McCafferty
Charlie and Heidi Buying Ice Cream (2006)
Textile/Print/Hand-stitching

Sophie Wightman
Girl on Holiday (2006)
Pen/Pencil

Matthew Hollister
Drugs (2005)
Ink on paper

Christopher King
Untitled (2006)
Pen/Ink/Adobe Photoshop

Christian Barthold
Streetgirl (2006)
India ink/Adobe Photoshop

Cybèle
Girl in Pasadena (2001)
Adobe Illustrator

Cecilia Carlstedt
Untitled, for *Damernas Värld* (2005)
Pencil/Adobe Photoshop

Marco Amitrano
Tina is Waiting (2005)
Adobe Photoshop/Discreet 3D Studio Max

Jason V Jaring
Vector_Chill (2006)
Adobe Illustrator

Jasper Sinchai Chadprajong
Johnny on Acid (2006)
Acrylic on corrugated
card/Coloured pencil/Ink

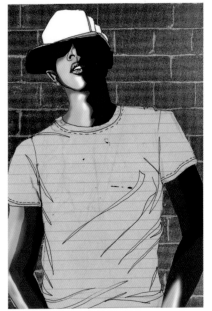

Helen Turner
Too Cool (2005)
Ink/Adobe
Photoshop

Nicholas Billiris
Streets Are
Watching (2005)
Adobe
Photoshop/Adobe
Illustrator

Alex Green
Greeting (2005)
Pencil/Pen/Paint/Collage/Ad
obe Photoshop

Lopetz:BD
3guys (2003)
Adobe Photoshop

Jacqui Paull and
Carl Melegari
Aaron (2004)
Adobe
Photoshop

Jacqui Paull and
Carl Melegari
Marc and Miu
(2004)
Adobe
Photoshop

Vincent Agostino
Smoking Skin (2006)
Acrylic

Emily Allen
Old Boy (2006)
Adobe Photoshop

Yurikov Kawahiro
Working with Music (2006)
Pencil/Adobe Photoshop

159

Yusuke Saitoh
Orson (2006)
Adobe Photoshop/Corel Painter

Arthur Mount
Jacket (2001)
Adobe Illustrator

Elena Lavdovskaya Konstantinovna
TSUM Menswear Campaign (2005)
Aquarelle/Ink/Adobe Photoshop

Jan Feindt
R.E.M. (2004)
Pen/Ink/Adobe Photoshop

Christopher Corr
Broadway NYC (2002)
Gouache

Elena Lavdovskaya Konstantinovna
TSUM Menswear Campaign (2005)
Aquarelle/Ink/Adobe Photoshop

Stuart Holmes
NY: Brooklyn (2005)
Adobe Illustrator

Masa
Trece (2003)
Adobe Illustrator

Stuart
Holmes
NY: Queens
(2005)
Adobe
Illustrator

Paul Watmough
We Know (2006)
Pen/Ink/Adobe Photoshop

Stuart Holmes
Do ya' Wanna? (2001)
Adobe Illustrator

Bil Donovan
Urban Warrior (1999)
Ink/Pastel/Graphite/
Gouache

Edel Rodriguez
Untitled (2005)
Pastel and ink on paper

Joseph S Arruda
The Weez (2005)
Adobe Photoshop/GNU
Image Manipulation
Program

Zed
Freddy Durst,
*Playboy* Magazine (2002)
Adobe Illustrator

Yusuke Saitoh
Positivity (2004)
Adobe
Photoshop/Corel
Painter

Jacqui Paull and Carl Melegari
Battersea Boy (2004)
Adobe Photoshop

Bil Donovan
Urban Guy (1998)
Graphite/Pastel/Gouache

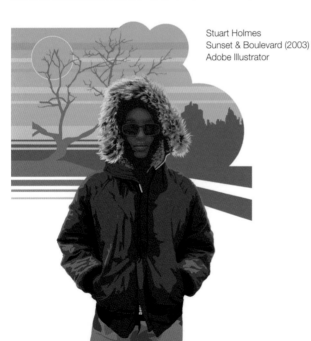

Stuart Holmes
Sunset & Boulevard (2003)
Adobe Illustrator

David Nwokedi
Moss Side Gang (2005)
Pencil/Watercolour/Adobe
Photoshop/Adobe Illustrator

Omar Buckley
Gettofab (2006)
Oil/Charcoal/Coloured pencil/Acrylic/
Adobe Photoshop/Adobe Illustrator

Oscar Gimenez
Inner City (2001)
Ink/Adobe Photoshop

Edel Rodriguez
The Roots (2005)
Pastel and ink on paper

Sarah Turner
Alternative Music Fan (2006)
Adobe Illustrator

171

Marco Amitrano
Standing at the Door (2004)
Adobe Photoshop

Laura Laine
Boy with Jacket (2006)
Pencil/Marker pen

Charlotte Willingale
Arthur (2006)
Pencil/Pen

Marco Amitrano
Duke Duke (2004)
Adobe Photoshop

Anna Saunders
Dance with
Michael (2005)
Watercolour
pencil/
Adobe
Photoshop

Shiho Matsubara
Rubbing Hands (2006)
Adobe Illustrator

Shiho Matsubara
Stretching (2006)
Adobe Illustrator

Elena Ambotaite
FALL, in Love (2006)
Pen/Adobe Photoshop

Madeleine Egremont
Young London (2006)
Pencil/Pen/Ink/Adobe Photoshop

Stuart Holmes
East LDN – Millennium Generation (2001)
Adobe Illustrator

Wayne Murray
Young Love? (2004)
Pencil/Adobe Illustrator

Oscar Gimenez
Shopping (2004)
Ink/Adobe Photoshop

Lior Yefet Tabib
Young Couple (2005)
Adobe Photoshop/Macromedia FreeHand

Yumiko Kayukawa
Mii Ando Mai Beibi
(Me and My Baby) (2003)
Acrylic and ink on illustration board

# Children

babies    toddlers&tots    juniors    tweenies    teens

Wai
Juggling (2004)
Adobe Illustrator/Adobe Photoshop

Annabelle J Verhoye
Diary of a Father (2003)
Chine collé/Adobe Photoshop

Nancy Davis
Mother and
Child (2002)
Macromedia
FreeHand

Dorothea Renault
Baby Spa (2004)
Adobe Illustrator

Sally Pring
Four in a Bed (2005)
Pencil/Collage/Adobe Photoshop

Tobias Wandres
Untitled (2003)
Macromedia FreeHand

Annabelle J Verhoye
The Beginning (2005)
Chine collé/Adobe Photoshop

Christiane Engel
Gwyneth (2006)
Pen/Ink/Collage

Yumiko Kayukawa
Gosai (Five Years Old) (2005)
Acrylic and ink on canvas

Christiane Engel
Baby on Futon (2005)
Oil pastel/Collage

Mark Borgions
Cut Out Max (2005)
Adobe Photoshop/Adobe Illustrator/Corel Painter

Tobias Wandres
Untitled (2004)
Macromedia FreeHand

Christiane Engel
Fancy Dress Party (2005)
Oil pastel/Pencil/Collage

Jacquie O'Neill
Summer Cycling (2005)
Adobe Illustrator

Sholto Walker
Scooter Girl (2006)
Ink on paper/Adobe
Illustrator

Claire Ann Baker
Little Star (2005)
Vintage photo
collage/Gouache/
Found objects

Claire Ann Baker
Grand Fellow (2003)
Vintage photo
collage/Gouache/Found objects

Kristie Jarita Lathbury
Sweet Bamboo (2006)
Adobe Illustrator

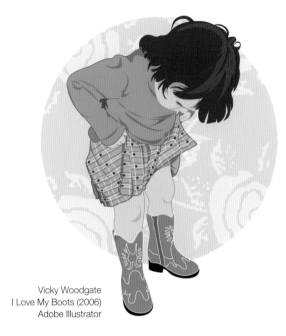

Vicky Woodgate
I Love My Boots (2006)
Adobe Illustrator

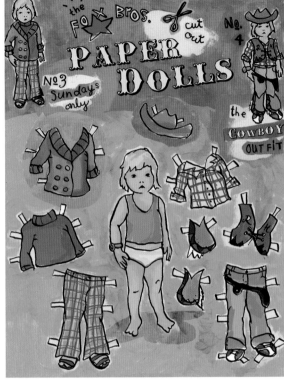

Christiane Engel
Fox Bros Paperdolls (2005)
Pen/Ink/Collage

Vicky Woodgate
Princess for a Day (2006)
Adobe Illustrator

Sarah Beetson
Dress Up Like Mummy: Alanis,
Abbie, Alice (2002)
Mixed media on wood

Asako Masunouchi
Fun Fun (2005)
Adobe Photoshop

Vicky Woodgate
Untitled (2006)
Adobe Illustrator

Michael Frith
Frieda (1997)
Watercolour

Rian Hughes
Friends Together (2004)
Adobe Illustrator/Adobe
Photoshop

Kim Longhurst
I Dream of Pretty, Happy Things (2001)
Macromedia FreeHand/Adobe Photoshop

Charlotte
Backhouse
Black Book (2006)
Ink/Spray
paint/Adobe
Photoshop

Yejin Yoon
Joy Box (2005)
Adobe Photoshop

Christiane Engel
Rude Beaver (2005)
Acrylic/Pen/Ink/Collage

Christiane Engel
Cheeky Fish (2005)
Acrylic/Pen/Ink/Collage

Lucy Allen
Woo Hoo! (2005)
Ink pen/Adobe Photoshop

Christy McCaffrey
Punk Rock Girl (2003)
Cut paper

Yejin Yoon
Hallo! (2005)
Adobe Photoshop

Christy McCaffrey
Seniors (2003)
Cut paper

Jacquie O'Neill
It Wasn't Me (2005)
Adobe Illustrator

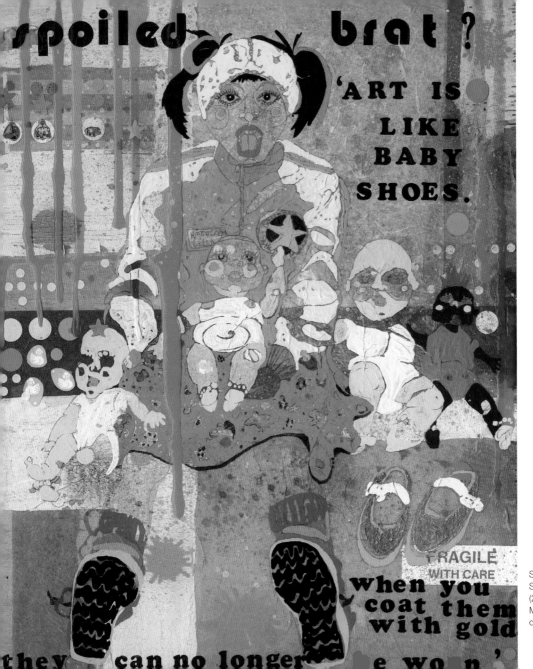

Sarah Beetson
Spoiled Brat
(2004)
Mixed media
on wood

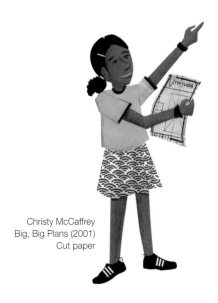

Christy McCaffrey
Big, Big Plans (2001)
Cut paper

Christy McCaffrey
Frosh (2001)
Cut paper

Christy McCaffrey
Indie Links (2001)
Cut paper

Karen Wegehenkel
Confirmation – Coming
of Age (2002)
Adobe Illustrator

Arturo Elena
Untitled, for Custo Barcelona (2003)
Ink/Felt tip pen

Yihsin Wu
An Odd Moment 2 (2005)
Pencil/Collage/Acrylic/Adobe Photoshop

Laerke Melgaard Hansen
Girl Juggling (2006)
Pen

Jacquie O'Neill
Summer Skipping (2005)
Adobe Illustrator

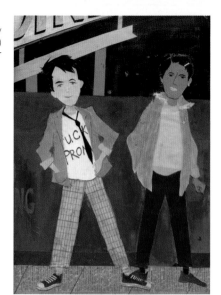

Christy McCaffrey
@#*$ Prom (2004)
Cut paper

Marina A
Townsend
Paperboy
(2002)
Charcoal

Hayato Jome
Kei (2004)
Acrylic/Adobe
Photoshop

Yihsin Wu
Fighting (2006)
Pencil/Collage
/Acrylic/Adobe
Photoshop

David Shephard
Graffiti Boy (2005)
Pen/Adobe Photoshop

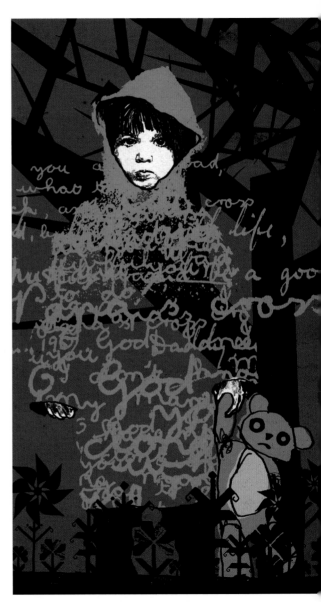

Paul Willoughby
Childhood Memoirs (2005)
Pencil/Found imagery/
Adobe Photoshop

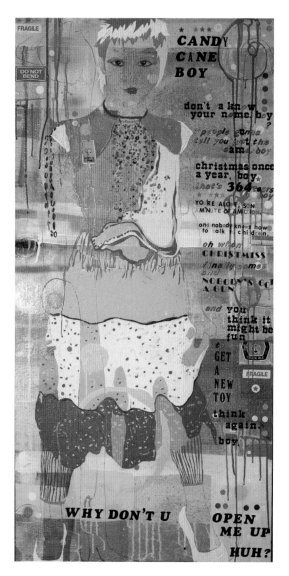

Sarah Beetson
Mail Order Boys – Candy Cane Boy (2004)
Mixed media on wood

Matthew Hollister
Portrait of XTC (2004)
Ink on paper

Christopher King
Anti (2004)
Pencil

Yihsin Wu
An Odd Moment 1 (2005)
Pencil/Collage/Acrylic/
Adobe Photoshop

Varshesh Joshi
Untitled (2004)
Pencil/Ink/Macromedia FreeHand/
Adobe Flash/Adobe Photoshop

Wayne Murray
Smiler (2005)
Pencil/Adobe Illustrator

Asako Masunouchi
I'll Write to you Soon (2005)
Coloured pencil

Wayne Murray
Wheelie (2005)
Pencil/Adobe
Illustrator

Christy McCaffrey
Professional What?
(2004)
Cut paper

Daniel Chen
First Day (2005)
Macromedia
FreeHand/Adobe
Photoshop

Christy McCaffrey
Sophomores (2004)
Cut paper

Charlotte Sophie Backhouse
Trinkets (2006)
Pen/Ink/Adobe Photoshop

James Burns
Brigid Rose (2000)
Adobe Illustrator

Margat Aurélie
Adonescance
n*1 (2005)
Collage/Ink/Oil
pastel

Margat Aurélie
Adonescance
n*2 (2005)
Collage/Ink/Oil
pastel

Claudio Parentela
Untitled (2005)
Ink and pen on paper

Hannah Broadway
Shopping (2006)

Raissa Gabriel
Buddy Up (2006)
Ink/Marker pen

Bella Pilar
Mom's Closet (2005)
Gouache

Bella Pilar
Grey Art (2005)
Gouache

Hayato Jome
Zushiban Guard of Feretory
(2003)
Acrylic on paper

Rhiannon Cunag
Rapunzel (2005)
Adobe Illustrator

Helen Turner
Lily (2003)
Ink/Adobe Photoshop

Claudio Parentela
Untitled (2005)
Ink and pen on paper

David Nwokedi
What Does Your Soul Look Like? (2006)
Pencil/Watercolour/Adobe
Photoshop/Adobe Illustrator

Ekua Doduwa Akumanyi
Hattie (2003)
Ink pen/Adobe Photoshop

Jeeyun Lee
Girl in Red (2005)
Watercolour

Tiffany Lynch
Interior Birds (2005)
Pen/Ink/Adobe Photoshop

Hayato Jome
Pier Pace (2003)
Acrylic on paper

Rhiannon Cunag
Love at First Sight (2005)
Adobe Illustrator

Jens Rotzsche
Vintage of '88 (2005)
Adobe Illustrator

Marguerite Sauvage
University Coming Soon, What Choice... (2005)
Pencil/Adobe Photoshop

Christian Barthold
I Hate You! (2004)
India ink/Adobe Photoshop

Stuart Holmes
Teens, MET Police website (2006)
Adobe Illustrator

Meirav Shaul
Alon in Blue (2006)
Acrylic on paper

Claire Townsend
Casual Attitude (2006)
Watercolour/Ink

Sarah Beetson
The New Music Revolution – Scratch My Record (2005)
Mixed media on wood

Naomi Austin
Playin' It Cool (2004)
Adobe Illustrator

Medeleine Egremont
Relax (2005)
Pencil/Pen/Ink/Adobe Photoshop

Hayato Jome
Etude of Field Rose (2001)
Acrylic on paper

Yumiko Kayukawa
Kamofuraaju
(Camouflage) (2003)
Acrylic and ink on
illustration board

Kun-Sung Chung
Tokyo Girl (2006)
Adobe Illustrator

Yuko Shimizu
Untitled, *The Village Voice*
(2003)
Ink/Adobe Photoshop

Asako Masunouchi
Make Her Envy (2005)
Coloured pencil

Lopetz:BD
Raincoat (2003)
Adobe Photoshop

Robert Weiss
Gothic Lolita (2006)
Adobe Illustrator

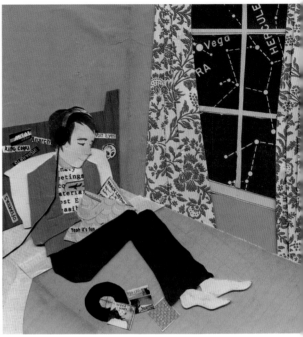

Christy McCaffrey
Radio, Radio (2005)
Cut paper

Daniel Chen
My Time (2005)
Macromedia FreeHand/Adobe Photoshop

Rian Hughes
Bootleg (2005)
Adobe Illustrator/Adobe Photoshop

Javier Joaquin
Dancing in the Street (2005)
Adobe Illustrator

Katie Wood
Embarrassing Moment: Rollerblades (2005)
Adobe Photoshop

Jacqui Paull and Carl Melegari
Looking-out (2003)
Adobe Photoshop

Madeleine Egremont
Skate Park (2006)
Pencil/Pen/Ink/Adobe Photoshop

Jacqui Paull and Carl Melegari
The Grind (2003)
Adobe Photoshop

# Sport and Leisure

gym   track   ballgames   snow&ice

blades&boards   biking   aquatics

Martina Farrow
Express (2003)
Adobe Illustrator

Christian Barthold
Fitness (2005)
India ink/Gouache/Adobe
Photoshop

James Burns
Yoga (2004)
Adobe Illustrator

Christian Barthold
Sports (2005)
India ink/Gouache/Adobe Photoshop

Annabelle J Verhoye
Indulge Yourself (2003)
Chine collé/Adobe Photoshop

Jason O'Malley
Locker Room (2006)
Adobe Illustrator

Martina Farrow
Ban Cellulite (2004)
Adobe Illustrator

Kun-Sung Chung
Jogging Girl (2005)
Adobe Illustrator

Tanya Unger
Ballerina (2006)
Adobe Illustrator

Hayato Jome
Shujinko – Hero in You (2001)
Acrylic on paper

235

Daniel Mackie
Get Down and Give
Me 10 (2004)
Pencil/Adobe
Photoshop

Jason O'Malley
Sexy Massage (2006)
Adobe Illustrator

Vincent Agostino
Weight Training Series (2004)
Clockwise from top left: Squats;
Press Ups; Dumb Bell Lifts; Dumb
Bell Curls
Acrylic

Gavin Reece
Morning Run (2004)
Adobe Photoshop

Oscar Gimenez
Needing a Massage? (2004)
Pencil/Adobe Photoshop

Monica Laita
NY Estate Agency N.3 (2006)
Adobe Photoshop

Lee Woodgate
How to ... Finish (2005)
Adobe Photoshop

Jonathan Williams
50/50 Ball (2005)
Pencil/Adobe Photoshop

Naomi Austin
Heading for Glory (2006)
Adobe Illustrator

Iván Solbes Canales
Football Day! (2004)
Ink/Paper/Macromedia FreeHand/Adobe Photoshop

Nick Larrett
Jack, Waiting
(2003)
Adobe Photoshop

241

Nicholas Billiris
Rebirth of Slick (2006)
Adobe Photoshop/Adobe Illustrator

Borja Uriarte
Rugby Player (2005)
Fabric

Marco Gallotta
Urban Play (2006)
Linocut/Photography/Adobe Photoshop

Julian Kloster
Court Practice Gear (2005)
Adobe Photoshop/Adobe Illustrator

Michael Crampton
Ski Poster (2003)
Gouache

Nicoletta Mazzesi
Skier (2004)
Adobe Photoshop/Adobe Illustrator

Jens Rotzsche
Glacial Suntan (2005)
Adobe Illustrator

Jens Rotzsche
The Alpinator (2005)
Adobe Illustrator

Arthur Mount
Jeremy Bloom (2005)
Adobe Illustrator

Megan Davidson
Powder Love (2006)
Adobe Illustrator/Adobe Photoshop

Sarah Beetson
Ellesse – Downhill Skiing (2002)
Acrylic and gouache on paper

Sarah Beetson
Ellesse – Slalom Skiing (2002)
Acrylic and gouache on paper

Pinglet
Aspen (2002)
Adobe Illustrator

Jens Rotzsche
Aprés Ski Scheme (2005)
Adobe Illustrator

Nina Jensen-Collman
Après Ski (2006)
Collage

Nina Jensen-Collman
Monochrome (2006)
Collage

Bella Pilar
Ice Skating (2005)
Gouache

Elena Ambotaite
Catch Me if you Can (2006)
Pen/Adobe Photoshop

Lulu
Somerset House Ice Rink, London (2002)
Adobe Illustrator

Belicta Castelbarco
Davos (2005)
Ink/Watercolour

Arturo Elena
Capricorn, for Cosmopolitan, Spain (2004)
Ink/Felt tip pen

Rian Hughes
Jet Set Radio Future (2002)
Adobe Illustrator/Adobe Photoshop

Jacqui Paull and Carl Melegari
Erik (2005)
Adobe Photoshop

Giulio Iurissevich
Skates (2005)
Adobe Illustrator

Christian Barthold
Jump (2006)
India ink/Gouache/Adobe Photoshop

Coburn
Snowboarder (2006)
Adobe Illustrator

Christian Barthold
Skater (2006)
India ink/Gouache/Adobe Photoshop

Lucy Allen
Skateboard Widow (2005)
Ink pen/Adobe Photoshop

Michael
Crampton
BMX Cyclist
(2005)
Gouache

Herman Yap
Action Guy for Nivea Men, Singapore (2005)
Macromedia FreeHand/Adobe Photoshop

Jonathan Williams
Biker Chef at the Embassy Hotel (2003)
Pencil/Adobe Photoshop

Amy De Wolfe
Bike Ride (2005)
Adobe Illustrator

Jennie Yip
Adidas Sports (2006)
Coloured pencil on paper

Christian Barthold
Hellbiker (2006)
India ink/Adobe Photoshop/Adobe Illustrator

Yuko Yoshioka
Aller Contre le Vent (2006)
Adobe Photoshop

Dorothea Renault
Summer 2005 (2005)
Adobe Illustrator

Herman Yap
Beach Girl (2005)
Macromedia FreeHand/Adobe Photoshop

Symbolon
Swim (2005)
Adobe Illustrator

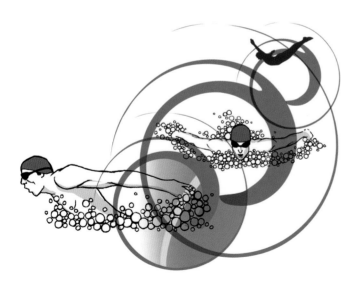

Oscar Gimenez
Swim! (2005)
Pencil/Adobe Photoshop

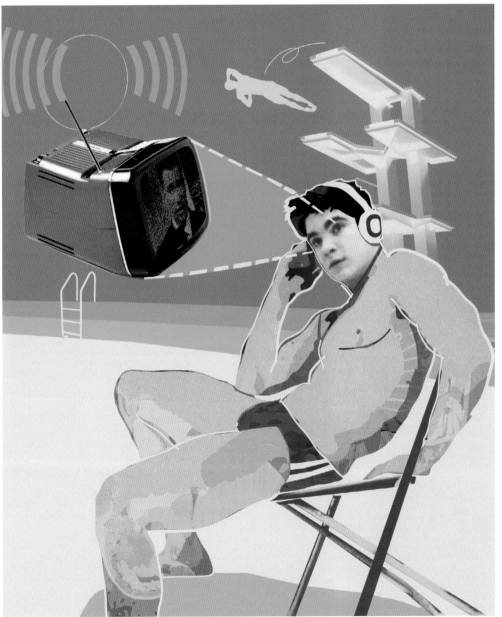

Andy Potts
Alexandre
Despatie (2005)
Pencil/Paint/Adobe
Photoshop/Adobe
Illustrator

Jason O'Malley
Beach Boy (2005)
Adobe Illustrator

Herman Yap
Sunseeker for
Nivea Men,
Singapore (2005)
Macromedia
FreeHand/Adobe
Photoshop

Leonid Gurevich
Surfer (2006)
en/Ink/Marker pen

Monsieur Z
Swiss Girls (2005)
Adobe Illustrator

Leonid Gurevich
Lucas (2006)
Pen/Ink/Marker pen

Megan Davidson
Polka-dot Bikini (2005)
Adobe Illustrator/Adobe Photoshop

Malena Gagliesi
Enjoying the Beach Alone,
BAMetropolis, 'Holidays: 86
Things to Do' (2005)
Adobe Illustrator

Christiane Engel
Sunburn (2005)
Oil pastel/Pencil/Collage

Andrew Bawidamann
Beach Ball Girl (2004)
Adobe Illustrator

Jens Rotzsche
Siren of Suntan (2006)
Adobe Illustrator

Nicoletta Mazzesi
Summertime (2004)
Adobe Photoshop/Adobe Illustrator

Stuart Holmes
Beach Veranda (2002)
Adobe Illustrator

Fiona Maclean
Bondi Bikini
Babe (2005)
Adobe
Illustrator

Marcella
Peluffo
Flower Bikini
(2006)
Corel Painter

Kristie Jarita Lathbury
Hot Beach (2006)
Adobe Illustrator

Yusuke Saitoh
On the Beach (2006)
Adobe Photoshop/Corel Painter

Christophe Lardot
Dans Les Champs (2006)
Adobe Photoshop

Ekaterina Matveeva
Summer Cocktail (2006)
Wacom Cintiq/Adobe Photoshop/Adobe Illustrator

LiXian Teng
Beach Chic (2006)
Adobe Illustrator

Cecilia Carlstedt
Untitled, *Mall* Magazine (2006)
Pencil/Adobe Photoshop

Marsha Silvestri
Surf Tank and Trunk with Dragons (2002)
Charcoal/Adobe Photoshop/Adobe Illustrator

Tina Berning
Über wasser (2002)
Ball pen/Vector Graphic/
OCD paper/Adobe Photoshop

Tina Berning
Unter wasser
(2002)
Ball
pen/Vector
Graphic/
OCD
paper/Adobe
Photoshop

Claudio Parentela
Untitled (2005)
Ink and pen on paper

Stina Persson
Tourist (2003)
Ink/Mexican cut papers/Adobe photoshop

John Jay Cabuay
Thongs in the Sun (2006)
Pen/Ink/Adobe Photoshop

Zed
C&A Swimwear (2002)
Adobe Illustrator

Kerstin Wacker
Beach (2006)
Pen/Watercolour/Adobe Photoshop

Marie Gibson
Giraffe Woman
(2005)
Photograph/F
abric collage

Claire Ann Baker
2 Swimmers (2006)
Mixed media/Vintage fabrics/Paper/Photo transfer/Hand stitch

Cecilia Carlstedt
Damernas Värld (2004)
Pencil/Adobe Illustrator

Katherine Prange
Untitled (2005)
Plastic beads

# Accessories

footwear   bags   headwear   eyewear

jewellery   techno   umbrellas

Maria Cardelli
Shoe Shopping (2000)
Adobe Photoshop

Marcos Chin
The Cost of a Fab Life (2004)
Adobe Illustrator

Sherill Gross
Beauty Ritual #10 (2006)
Paper

Laura McCafferty
Mel on the Dancefloor at 2am (2005)
Textile/Print/Hand-stitching

Lys Wilcox
Mary Jane (2003)
Beads/Fabric/Collage

Lys Wilcox
Slipper (2003)
Collage/Taffeta fabric paper

Lys Wilcox
Spectator Pump (2003)
Collage/Fabric paper

Martina Farrow
Shoe Shop (2003)
Adobe Illustrator

Zachariah O'Hora
Float Like a Butterfly (2005)
Acrylic on board

Bella Pilar
Floral Skirt (2004)
Gouache

Matthew Hollister
Spoils (2004)
Ink on paper

Janet Pui Kee Lui
My Fairytale Collection: Phoenix (2005)
Photocopy/Adobe Photoshop/Adobe Illustrator

Janet Pui Kee Lui
My Fairytale Collection: Forest (2005)
Photocopy/Adobe Photoshop/Adobe Illustrator

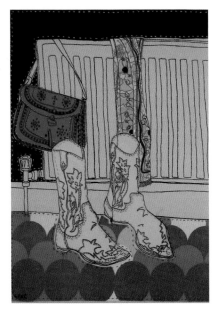

Laura
McCafferty
Cowgirl Boots
(2006)
Textile/Print/
Hand-stitching

Erica Sharp
Green Boots
(2005)
Adobe
Photoshop

Kari Modén
Boots (2005)
Adobe
Illustrator

Christiane Engel
Sushi Boots (2005)
Pen/Ink/Acrylic

Louise Alexander
Pitter Patter (2005)
Pencil/Adobe Photoshop

Kun-Sung Chung
Ego Booster, How to be an Irresistible
Woman, Carlton Books (2005)
Adobe Illustrator

Louise Alexander
YeeHa (2004)
Pencil/Collage/
Adobe Photoshop

James Burns
Shoes (2003)
Adobe Illustrator

Kat Devine
Put Your Shoes On (2005)
Acrylic/Ink/Embroidery on cotton

Jonas Bergstrand
Shoes (2005)
Adobe Illustrator/Adobe
Photoshop

Kari Modén
Sneakers, *Jack* magazine (2004)
Adobe Illustrator

Kari Modén
Sneakers, *Jack* magazine (2004)
Adobe Illustrator

Scott Wills
Denim Boot (2003)
Adobe Photoshop

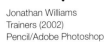

Jonathan Williams
Trainers (2002)
Pencil/Adobe Photoshop

Fhiona
Galloway
Bees (2006)
Macromedia
FreeHand

Iván Solbes
Canales
Turismo de Suelos
(2004)
Ink/Paper/
Macromedia
FreeHand/Adobe
Photoshop

Iván Solbes
Canales
Sol Solero
(2004)
Ink/Paper/
Macromedia
FreeHand/
Adobe
Photoshop

Iván Solbes
Canales
Sales (2004)
Ink/Paper/
Macromedia
FreeHand/
Adobe
Photoshop

Lucy Truman
Shopaholic (2004)
Corel Painter/Corel
Draw

Malena Gagliesi
Buenos Aires Street Fashion: Golden Leaves
Bag, *BAMetropolis* (2006)
Adobe Illustrator

Tania Howells
Heel Boy (2004)
Ink

Tania Howells
Tweed (2004)
Ink

Malena Gagliesi
Buenos Aires Street
Fashion: Pointy Shoes,
*BAMetropolis* (2006)
Adobe Illustrator

Arturo Elena
Untitled, for
*Cosmopolitan*, Spain
(2002)
Ink/Felt tip pen

Arturo Elena
Untitled, for
*Cosmopolitan*, Spain
(2002)
Ink/Felt tip pen

Gillian Cook
Handbag and Shoes (2006)
Adobe Photoshop

Yolanda Gonzalez
Flower Dress (2005)
Gouache on paper

Alessandra Scandella
Lady in Blue (2005)
Corel Painter/Adobe Photoshop

Yuko Shimizu
Untitled, *The Village Voice* (2002)
Ink/Adobe Photoshop

Sam Wilson
I Love Shopping (2006)
Paint/Crayon/Ink/Collage/Adobe Photoshop

Stina Persson
Shopping (2002)
Watercolour dyes/Ink/
Adobe Photoshop

Pinglet
Messenger
(2002)
Adobe
Illustrator

Marcos Chin
Cool Gifts (2005)
Adobe Illustrator

Gavin Reece
Trolley Chic
(2005)
Adobe
Photoshop

Yuko Shimizu
Untitled, *Chow*
Magazine
(2005)
Ink/Adobe
Photoshop

Jason O'Malley
Bags for Men (2004)
Adobe Illustrator

Carlo Stanga
NY Run (2004)
Adobe Photoshop

Kyra Kendall
Nap (2006)
Adobe Illustrator

Sonya Suhariyan
Florescence (2005)
Gouache/Acrylic/Felt tip pen

Pinglet
Gatehold (2002)
Adobe Illustrator

Pascale Evrard
Autumn Man (2006)
Ink/Watercolour/Pencil/Adobe Photoshop

Kim Rosen
The Academic (2004)
Ink/Acrylic/Adobe Photoshop

Claire Anderson
Nancy (2005)
Stitched cotton thread on calico

John Prikryl
Bag Program (2005)
Sketchpad/Adobe Photoshop/Adobe Illustrator

Kyra Kendall
Spender (2006)
Adobe Illustrator

Nina Edwards
Shop Girl (2006)
Adobe Illustrator

Bella Pilar
Yorkie (2004)
Gouache

Amparo Losana
Longchamp for *Elle* magazine (2004)
Watercolour

Wai
Windy (2006)
Adobe Illustrator/Adobe Photoshop

Stuart Holmes
Spring Has
Sprung (2002)
Adobe
Illustrator

Lulu
Summertime
(2003)
Adobe
Illustrator

Sofia Dias
Nudity (2005)
Macromedia
FreeHand

Maria Cardelli
Horse Race,
*The Times*
(2002)
Adobe
Photoshop

Giulio Iurissevich
Paris Lounge (2003)
Macromedia FreeHand/Adobe Illustrator

Henry Obasi
Kangol Autumn/Winter, Snow Lovers (2006)
Adobe Photoshop/Adobe Illustrator/Paint/Ink

Henry Obasi
Kangol Spring/Summer (2005)
Adobe Photoshop/Adobe
Illustrator/Paint/Ink

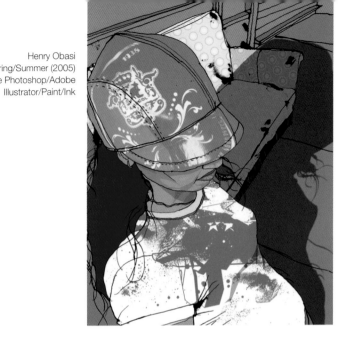

Anna Saunders
Work Just a Little (2005)
Watercolour pencil/Adobe
Photoshop

Chenna
Kangol Spring Summer (2005)
Ink/Spray paint/Charcoal/Pencil/
Adobe Photoshop

Anton Storey
Electronic (2004)
Pen/Adobe Photoshop

Arthur Mount
Larry (2005)
Adobe Illustrator

Henry Obasi
Kangol Autumn/Winter, Snow Hunter
(2006)
Adobe Photoshop/Adobe
Illustrator/Paint/Ink

Jonathan Williams
Things You Shouldn't Do Over
the Age of 30: Wear a Kangol
Hat (2003)
Pencil/Adobe Photoshop

Wai
Spring (2005)
Adobe
Illustrator/
Adobe
Photoshop

Hannah Broadway
Chanel Sunglasses (2006)
Fine liner/Adobe Photoshop

Hannah
Broadway
Looking Pretty
Cool (2006)
Fine
liner/Adobe
Photoshop

Hannah Broadway
Felix Wears Glasses (2006)
Biro/Adobe Photoshop

Taryn Lee
Jak (jakandjil.com) (2006)
Adobe Illustrator

Wai
Reflection
(2005)
Adobe
Illustrator/
Adobe
Photoshop

Maria Cardelli
Taurus, Vital
Magazine (2000)
Adobe Photoshop

Aga Baranska
Drama (2006)
Collage/Paint/
Adobe
Photoshop

Maria Cardelli
Accessories,
Telecom
(2001)
Adobe
Photoshop

Kenneth
Andersson
Shades (2005)
Ink/Adobe
Illustrator

Jason
O'Malley
Hipster
Eyewear
(2006)
Adobe
Illustrator

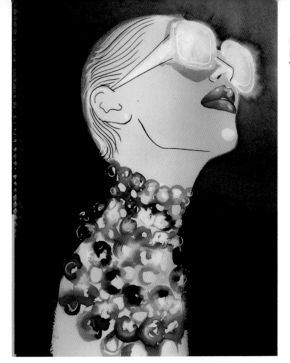

Margot Mace van Huijkelom
Lady with Glasses (2006)
Watercolour/Ink pen

Pierre-Paul Pariseau
Waiting for Marcello (2005)
Adobe Photoshop

Natascha Engelmann
Silhouette II (2000)
Pencil/Watercolour/Adobe
Photoshop/Adobe Illustrator

Erica Glasier
Valentine (2003)
Adobe Photoshop/Adobe
Illustrator

Natascha Engelmann
Silhouette I (2000)
Pencil/Watercolour/Adobe
Photoshop/Adobe Illustrator

Erica Glasier
Engaged (2003)
Adobe Photoshop/Adobe
Illustrator

Pinglet
Jade (2002)
Adobe Illustrator

Pinglet
Goldie (2002)
Adobe Illustrator

Wai
Drop (2005)
Adobe Illustrator/
Adobe Photoshop

Belicta Castelbarco
Black Lady (2005)
Ink/Adobe Photoshop

Sherill Gross
Beauty Ritual #11 (2006)
Paper

Rob Arnow
Untitled (1998)
Adobe Photoshop

Ewa Brockway
Pink Pearls (2005)
Adobe Photoshop

Amy De Wolfe
Spotted (2006)
Adobe Illustrator

Ewa Brockway
Power of Beauty (2005)
Adobe Photoshop

Menisha
St Valentine
(2006)
Adobe
Photoshop

Anna Tuomaala
and Natalie Eley
Kate (2005)
Pencil/Adobe
Photoshop

Anna Tuomaala
and Natalie Eley
Natasha (2005)
Pencil/Adobe
Photoshop

Steph Dix
Hazy Jane (2005)
Pencil/Adobe Photoshop

Anna
Tuomaala and
Natalie Eley
Christy (2005)
Pencil/Adobe
Photoshop

Tina Berning
Herzblut (2004)
Watercolour/Pen/
Adobe Photoshop

Lucy Truman
Oh Boy! (2005)
Corel Painter

Javier Joaquin
My Desk (2004)
Adobe Illustrator

Sonya Suhariyan
Love in the Cover (2005)
Gouache/Acrylic/Felt tip pen

Alex Green
Playtime (2005)
Pencil/Paint/Pen/
Collage/Adobe Photoshop

Cecilia Carlstedt
Untitled, *Bon* Magazine (2005)
Pencil/Adobe Illustrator/Adobe Photoshop

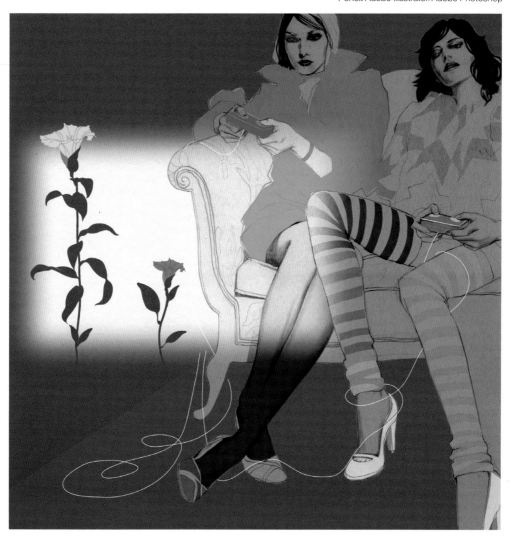

Sofia Dias
Digital Attitude
(2004)
Macromedia
FreeHand

Herman Yap
Summer Headphones (2002)
Macromedia FreeHand/Adobe Photoshop

Kim Rosen
Average Student
(2004)
Ink/Acrylic/Adobe
Photoshop

Sarah Turner
Mod Listening to
Music (2006)
Adobe Illustrator

Monica Hellström
iPod Girl (2005)
Pencil/Brush/Adobe
Photoshop

Jacqui Paull
and Carl
Melegari
Hip Hop
(2004)
Adobe
Photoshop

Xing Jun Long
Want Some Apple? (2005)
Adobe Photoshop

Georgina Fearns
Football Mum (2005)
Ink on paper/Adobe
Photoshop

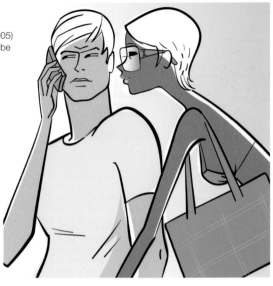

Dorothea
Renault
Couple (2005)
Adobe
Illustrator

Astrid Mueller (Potatomammadesign)
Lucy (2006)
Corel Painter

Malena Gagliesi
Personal Stationary Card:
Malala Fontan,
Photographer (2004)
Adobe Illustrator

Daniel Chen
Girl Talk (2005)
Macromedia FreeHand/Adobe
Photoshop

Arthur Mount
Cyber Shot (2003)
Adobe Illustrator

Monica Laita
Architech N.3 (2006)
Adobe Photoshop

Nina Edwards
Metropolitan Miss (2004)
Adobe Illustrator/Adobe Photoshop

Wai
Late (2006)
Adobe
Illustrator/
Adobe
Photoshop

Yuko Shimizu
Untitled, *The Village
Voice* (2003)
Ink/Adobe Photoshop

Helen James
Fashion Victim (2005)
Adobe Photoshop

# Beauty and Glamour

grooming   cosmetics   make-up   hair

eye candy   hunks

Kosmas Apatangelos (artist)
Stephan Freund (photographer)
Glam of Sorrow (2006)
Adobe Illustrator/Adobe Photoshop

Jens Rotzsche
Early Risers (2006)
Adobe Illustrator

Christopher Corr
Clean Guy (2003)
Gouache

Wai
Aquarius
(2006)
Adobe
Illustrator/
Adobe
Photoshop

J David McKenney
Rinse (2005)
Ink/Adobe Photoshop

Sherill Gross
Beauty Ritual #4 (2005)
Paper

Edel Rodriguez
Nine Songs (2005)
Oil-based ink on paper/Adobe Photoshop

Vincent Agostino
Shaving Tips (2006)
Acrylic

Louise Alexander
Nathan's Nails (2004)
Pencil

Wai
Beauty (2006)
Adobe Illustrator/
Adobe Photoshop

Christopher Corr
Clean Shave (2004)
Gouache

Jonathan
Williams
Blueface (2003)
Pencil/Adobe
Photoshop

Annika Wester
Make-up (2005)
Ink pen/Gouache

Helen Turner
Beauty Tools (2005)
Ink/Adobe Photoshop

Jens Rotzsche
A Sacrifice for Venus
(2006)
Adobe Illustrator

Yuko Shimizu
Untitled, *Financial Times* Magazine (2003)
Ink/Adobe Photoshop

Jeanne Detallante
Freddie's Cat 1 (2005)
Adobe Photoshop

Kari Modén
Brand New Day, *Vero*Moda
magazine (2006)
Adobe Illustrator

Jeanne Detallante
Freddie's Cat 2 (2005)
Adobe Photoshop

Sherill Gross
Beauty Ritual #7
(2005)
Paper

Kun-Sung Chung
Quick 'n' Easy,
*Let's Party!*,
Lobster Press
(2004)
Adobe Illustrator

Georgina Fearns
Pampered (2005)
Ink on
paper/Adobe
Photoshop

Bella Pilar
Applying Mascara (2004)
Gouache

Natascha Engelmann
Lashes (2005)
Pencil/Adobe Photoshop

Eleanor
Ferguson
Lips (2005)
Acrylic/Corel
Painter/
Adobe
Photoshop

Bella Pilar
Applying Lipstick
(2004)
Gouache

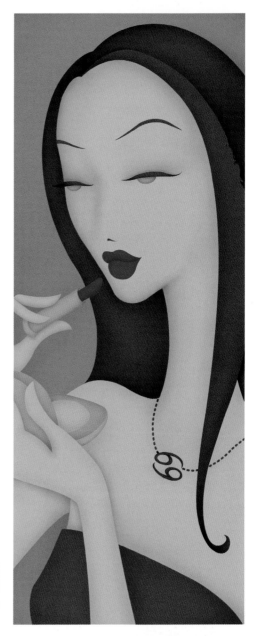

Wai
Lipstick (2004)
Adobe Illustrator/
Adobe Photoshop

Andrea
Wicklund
Conversation
(2004)
Acrylic/Ink

Sherill Gross
Beauty Ritual #8 (2005)
Paper

Diana Ponce
Jani Paris (2003)
Watercolour

Tanya Unger
Lovely Lip Gloss (2006)
Adobe Illustrator

Lucy Truman
Maybe She's Born
With It (2005)
Corel Painter

Bella Pilar
Nail Polish (2004)
Gouache

Lucy MacLeod
Thirties Girl (2006)
Charcoal/Adobe Photoshop

Lucy MacLeod
Rouge (2005)
Charcoal/Adobe Photoshop

Bella Pilar
Mascara (2004)
Gouache

Noumeda Carbone
R#3 (2005)
Ink

Noumeda Carbone
R#1 (2005)
Ink

Symbolon
Hair Care (2004)
Adobe Illustrator

Liz Lomax
Beauty Secrets (2004)
Acrylic and oil paint on Super Sculpey/Insulation
foam/Foamcore/Aluminium Foil/Adobe Photoshop

Malena Gagliesi
Beauty Steps, *Santo Buenos Aires* Agency (2006)
Adobe Illustrator

Cecilia Carlstedt
Virgo, for *Marie Claire* Magazine (2006)
Pencil/Adobe Photoshop

Yolanda Gonzales
Fro (1998)
Gouache on paper

Sherill Gross
Beauty Ritual #9 (2005)
Paper

Natascha Engelmann
Cut (2006)
Pencil/Watercolour/Adobe
Photoshop/Adobe Illustrator

Genevieve Kelly
Woman and Song Bird (2005)
Wallpaper/Collage/Photograph/Adobe Photoshop

Jennifer Berney
Queenie (2005)
Gouache/Pencil/Ink

Martina Farrow
Mischa (2005)
Adobe Illustrator

Stuart Holmes
Peek-a-boo! (2000)
Adobe Illustrator

Woonyoung Chang
Mirror, Don't Want to See
Myself (2006)
Micra pigma pen/Adobe
Photoshop

Kim Longhurst
Babylon (2005)
Macromedia
FreeHand/
Adobe Photoshop

Helen Turner
Hoops (2005)
Ink/Adobe Photoshop

Ekua Doduwa Akumanyi
Gyia (2005)
Ink pen/Adobe Photoshop

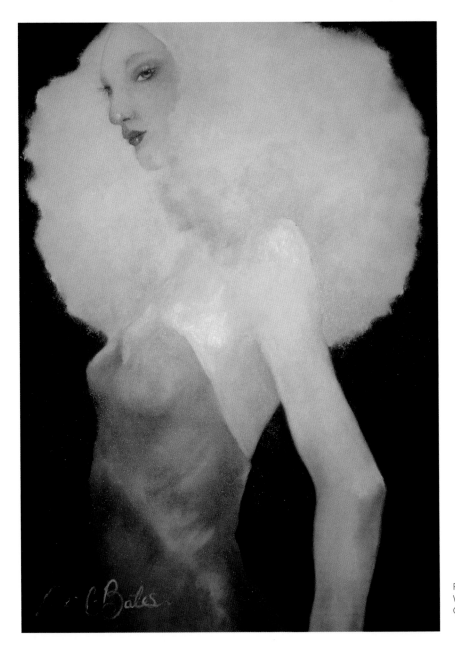

Pearl Bates
Winter Dreams (2005)
Oil on canvas

Steph Dix
Lily (2005)
Pencil/Adobe Photoshop

Ella Tjader
Madonna
(2005)
Adobe
Illustrator/
Adobe
Photoshop

Ella Tjader
Libra (2005)
Adobe Illustrator/
Adobe Photoshop

Ella Tjader
Mexican Bride
(2005)
Adobe
Illustrator/
Adobe
Photoshop

Ella Tjader
Scorpio (2005)
Adobe Illustrator/
Adobe Photoshop

Claire McMahon
Perfume (2006)
Adobe Photoshop/Adobe Illustrator

Lucy MacLeod
Scarlet Fever (2005)
Charcoal/Adobe Photoshop

Herman Yap
Midnight Magic (2005)
Macromedia FreeHand/Adobe Photoshop

Marguerite Sauvage
Swaroski Movie and Research (2005)
Pencil/Adobe Photoshop

Pearl Bates
Ebony (2005)
Oil on canvas

Giulio Iurissevich
Bellissima (2005)
Macromedia
FreeHand/Adobe
Photoshop/Adobe
Illustrator

Eric Bailey
Golden (2005)
Oil on Canvas

Carlos Maraz
Calendar Girl (2006)
Corel Painter

Ekua Doduwa
Akumanyi
Minky (2005)
Ink pen/Adobe
Photoshop

Kyra Kendall
Dancer (2006)
Adobe Illustrator

Wingnut Designs
Kiss Face (2005)
Traditional/Adobe Photoshop

Dilek Peker
Hypnose (2006)
Adobe Photoshop

Mats Bergen
Lace-up Leg (2005)
Adobe Photoshop/Adobe Illustrator

Juan Gonzalez
Ampa in the Nude (2005)
Gouache

Stuart Holmes
The Brown Room (2002)
Adobe Illustrator

Andrew Bawidamann
Love Bunny (2004)
Adobe Illustrator

Lulu
Mood (2005)
Adobe Illustrator

Lulu
Lola (2005)
Adobe Illustrator

Noumeda Carbone
R#4 (2006)
Ink/Adobe Photoshop

Woonyoung Chang
Femme Fatal of Swallowed Dream (2006)
Micra pigma pen/Adobe Photoshop

Fhiona Galloway
Red Lips (2005)
Macromedia FreeHand

J. David McKenney
Redhead (2005)
Ink/Adobe
Photoshop

Pinglet
Fetish (2002)
Adobe Illustrator

Erica Glasier
Fuuka Sakurai (2002)
Adobe Photoshop/Adobe Illustrator

Marie Gibson
Flamingo Lady (2005)
Photograph/Fabric collage

Bil Donovan
Pink Naomi (2003)
Ink

Jennifer Berney
Cabbage Butterfly (2006)
Gouache/Pencil/Ink

Marguerite Sauvage
Fire Girl Love You All (2005)
Pencil/Adobe Photoshop

Naomi Austin
Joey (2005)
Adobe Illustrator

Mel Simone Elliott
Cute Guy (2006)
Gouache/Adobe Illustrator

Irene Jacobs
Untitled, for *Man* magazine (2000)
Adobe Illustrator

Natascha Engelmann
Tattoo Boy I (2006)
Pencil/Adobe Photoshop

Monica Hellström
50 Cent (2005)
Pencil/Brush/Adobe Photoshop

Monsieur Z
Case Study
House 22 and
Boy (2005)
Adobe
Illustrator

Dilek Peker
Sexy Boy (2006)
Adobe Photoshop

Anna Saunders
I Stop and Stare (2006)
Watercolour pencil/Adobe
Photoshop

Koichi Fujii
Untitled (2005)
Adobe Illustrator

Kun-Sung Chung
Cool Guy (2006)
Adobe Photoshop/Adobe
Illustrator

Tobias Wandres
Untitled (2003)
Macromedia FreeHand

Wingnut Designs
Urban Cowboy (2005)
Traditional/Adobe Photoshop

Nick Larrett
Jim, Thinking (2005)
Adobe Photoshop

Arthur Mount
YSL (2003)
Adobe Illustrator

Natascha Engelmann
Tattoo Boy II (2006)
Pencil/Adobe Photoshop

Kristie Jarita Lathbury
Electric Blue (2006)
Adobe Illustrator

Jeff Mulawka
Rude Boy (2004)
Adobe Photoshop

Jan Feindt
Tricky (2002)
Pen/Ink/Adobe Photoshop

Jeff Mulawka
Flirt (2005)
Adobe Photoshop

Hélène Genevoix
Plurality (2004)
Adobe Photoshop

# ARTIST CONTACT DETAILS

**Agostino, Vincent**
email: atomic7@ihug.com.au
www.hottrashstudios.com
**Ahmadyar, Wahid**
email:
Wahid_Ahmadyar@hotmail.co.uk
**Akumanyi, Ekua Doduwa**
email: equaakum@btinternet.com
www.artwanted.com/strawberry
**Allen, Emily**
email: emily1allen@hotmail.co.uk
**Allen, Lucy**
email: lucyallen39@yahoo.co.uk
www.lucyallen.co.uk
**Alexander, Louise**
email: lou_alexander@hotmail.com
www.artshole.co.uk/louisealexander
**Ambotaite, Elena**
email: elena.ny@verizon.net
www.elenaambo.com
**Amitrano, Marco**
email: marcoxamitrano@yahoo.com
www.ArtWanted.com/marco.a
**Anderson, Claire**
email:
clairefrancesanderson@hotmail.com
**Andersson, Kenneth**
email: info@kennethandersson.com
www.kennethandersson.com
**Apatangelos, Kosmas**
email: kommigraphics@gmail.com
www.kommigraphics.gr
**Arnow, Rob**
email: design@robarnow.com
www.robarnow.com
**Arora, Harmind Singh**
email: harmind@gmail.com
www.artwanted.com/harmind
**Arruda, Joseph S.**
email: zeruch@vergenet.net
www.zeruch.net
zeruch.deviantart.com
**Aurélie, Margat**
email: margataurelie@hotmail.com
**Austin, Naomi**
email: naomi@naomiaustin.co.uk
www.naomiaustin.co.uk
**Austin, Paul**
email: austin_paul@hotmail.co.uk

**Backhouse, Charlotte Sophie**
email: lunadust@hotmail.com
**Bailey, Eric**
email: eric@birdsandbullets.com
www.birdsandbullets.com
**Baker, Claire Ann**
email: c.baker5@ntlworld.com
www.myspace.com/edithchick
**Baranska, Aga**
email: agabaranska@yahoo.com
www.agabaranska.com
www.eyecandy.co.uk
**Barthold, Christian**
email: weaverofyourdreams@gmx.de
christian-barthold.illustration.de
**Bates, Pearl**
email: info@pearlbates.com
www.pearlbates.com

**Bawidamann, Andrew**
email: andrew@bawidamann.com
www.bawidamann.com
**Beetson, Sarah**
email: sarahbeets@hotmail.com
Represented in Canada by
i2i Art Inc.
www.i2iart.com/Beetson
Represented in UK and rest of world
by Illustration Ltd
email: sarah@illustrationweb.com
www.illustrationweb.com
www.illustrationweb.com/
SarahBeetson
**Bergen, Mats**
email: matsbergen@t-online.de
www.matsbergen.com
Represented in Austria by
www.weinper.at
Represented in Asia by
www.ua-net.com
**Bergstrand, Jonas**
email: jonas@jonasbergstrand.com
www.jonasbergstrand.com
Represented by Central Illustration
email: info@centralillustration.com
www.centralillustration.com
**Berney, Jennifer**
email: jennifer_berney@yahoo.com

**Berning, Tina**
email: tina@tinaberning.de
Represented by CWC International
email: agent@cwc-i.com
www.cwc-i.com
Represented in Asia by Cross World
Connections
www.cwctokyo.com
**Billiris, Nicholas**
email: nbilliris@hotmail.com
**Boberg, Annie**
email: info@organisart.co.uk
www.organisart.co.uk
**Borgions, Mark**
email:
markborgions@handmademonsters.com
www.handmademonsters.com
**Broadway, Hannah**
email: Hbroadway@hotmail.com
www.number40.net/hannah.htm
**Brockway, Ewa**
email: ewaatusa@aol.com
www.ewabrockway.com
**Buckley, Omar**
email: URIN1234@yahoo.com
**Burns, James**
email: info@jamesburnsdesign.com
jamesburnsdesign.com
**Byrne, Andrea**
email: mail@andreabyrne.com
www.andreabyrne.com
**Byrne, Eva**
email: email@watsonspierman.com

**Cabuay, John Jay**
email: johnjay@johnjayart.com
www.johnjayart.com
Represented in USA by
Shannon Associates
email:
newyork@shannonassociates.com
**Canales, Iván Solbes**
email: ivan@ivansolbes.com
www.ivansolbes.com
**Cangialosi, Anna**
email: anna@annacangialosi.com
www.annacangialosi.com

**Carbone, Noumeda**
email: noumeda@tiscali.it
www.noumedacarbone.it
Represented by Private View
email: create@pvuk.com
www.pvuk.com
**Cardelli, Maria**
email: mcardelli-
illustrator@earthlink.net
Represented by Illustration Ltd
email: team@illustrationweb.com
www.illustrationweb.com/
MariaCardelli
**Carlstedt, Cecilia**
email: mail@ceciliacarlstedt.com
www.art-dept.com
www.agentbauer.com
www.ceciliacarlstedt.com
**Castelbarco, Belicta**
email: belicta@aol.com
Represented by Die Illustratoren
email: kontakt@illustratoren.de
www.illustratoren.de/
belictacastelbarco
**Chadprajong, Jasper Sinchai**
email: jasper_chad@hotmail.com
www.keep-quiet.com
**Chang, Woonyoung**
email: winnie76@gmail.com
eiti2.com/winnie
**Chen, Daniel**
Represented by i2i Art Inc
email: info@i2iart.com
www.i2iart.com
**Chenna**
Studio: PPAINT
email: chenna@ppaint.net
www.ppaint.net
Agent: UNIT
www.unit.nl
**Chin, Marcos**
email: marcos@marcoschin.com
www.marcoschin.com
**Chung, Kun-Sung**
email: info@kschung.com
www.kschung.com
**Coburn**
Represented by Meiklejohn
Illustration
email: info@meiklejohn.co.uk
www.meiklejohn.co.uk

**Cook, Gillian**
email: gillian@gilliancook.co.uk
www.gilliancook.co.uk
**Corr, Christopher**
email: Chris@Christophercorr.com
www.christophercorr.com
**Crampton, Michael**
Represented by Meiklejohn
Illustration
email: info@meiklejohn.co.uk
www.meiklejohn.co.uk
**Cunag, Rhiannon**
email: rhiannoncunag@gmail.com
rhiannoncunag.com
**Cybèle**
email: cybele@walkcycle.com
www.walkcycle.com
**Darama, Ulis**
email: ulisdarama@yahoo.com
**Davidson, Megan**
email: meg@megan-davidson.co.uk
www.megan-davidson.co.uk
**Davis, Nancy**
email: nandavis@cox.net
www.nancydavis.org
**de la Rosa, Cesar**
e-mail: BeleAmi@aol.com
www.CesardelaRosa.com
**de Wolfe, Amy**
email: amy@amydewolfe.com
www.amydewolfe.com
**Detallante, Jeanne**
email: jdetallante@gmail.com
www.jeannedetallante.com
Represented by ArtList Paris
email: jonathan@artlistparis.com
www.artlistparis.com
**Devil, Naomi**
email: naomidevil@naomidevil.com
www.naomidevil.com
**Devine, Kat**
email: kat_devine@hotmail.co.uk
**Dias, Sofia**
email: info@sofiadias.com
www.sofiadias.com
Represented by Pict UK
email: ukinfo@pict-web.com
www.pict-web.com
**Dix, Steph**
Represented by
Graham-Cameron Illustration
email: enquiry@graham-cameron
illustration.com
www.pictureprovider.com

**Docampo, Valeria**
email:
contacto@valeriadocampo.com.ar
www.valeriadocampo.com.ar/editorial
**Doerr, Maximilian**
email: Maximilian@6in7and8.com
www.6in7and8.com
**Donovan, Bil**
email: dukedonovan@earthlink.net
Represented by ArtCounsel Inc
artscounselinc.com

**Edwards, Nina**
email: nina@metropolitanmiss.com
www.portfolios.com/ninaedwards
www.metropolitanmiss.com
**Egremont, Madeleine**
email:
maddie@maddieegremont.com
**Elena, Arturo**
email: arturo@arturoelena.com
www.arturoelena.com
**Eley, Natalie**
email: nat_eley@yahoo.co.uk
**Elliott, Mel Simone**
email: mel.elliott@virgin.net
**Engel, Christiane**
email: chengel@gmx.net
www.desertfriends.com
**Engelmann, Natascha**
email: illustration@engelworld.com
www.engelworld.com
Represented by Kombinatrotweiss*
email: info@kombinatrotweiss.de
www.kombinatrotweiss.de
**Evrard, Pascale**
www.pascale-evrard.com
Represented by Illustrissimo
email: michel@illustrissmo.com
www.illustrissimo.com

**Farrow, Martina**
Represented by New Division
email: info@newdivision.com
www.newdivision.com
**Fearns, Georgina**
email: georgiefearns@hotmail.co.uk
**Feindt, Jan**
Represented in UK by Illustration Ltd
email: team@illustrationweb.com
www.illustrationweb.com/JanFeindt
**Ferguson, Eleanor**
email: lola_in_slacks@hotmail.com
www.artshole.co.uk/eleanorferguson.htm

**Freund, Stefan**
email: freund@stefanfreund.de
www.stefanfreund.de
**Frith, Michael**
email: info@michaelfrith.com
m.frith@lineone.net
www.michaelfrith.com
**Fujii, Koichi**
Represented in by Illustration Ltd
email: team@illustrationweb.com
www.illustrationweb.com/
KoichiFujii
**Furukawa, Koichiro**
email: koachen@hotmail.com

**Gabriel, Raissa**
email: raissa@raissagabriel.com
raissagabriel.com
**Gagliesi, Malena**
email: info@malenagagliesi.com.ar
www.malenagagliesi.com.ar
**Gallotta, Marco**
email: marcogallotta@yahoo.com
www.marcogallotta.com
**Galloway, Fhiona**
email: fg.illustration@virgin.net
**Genevoix, Helene**
email: thaniya@genevoix.com
**Gibson, Marie**
email: mariegibson_10@hotmail.com
**Gimenez, Oscar**
email: info@oscargimenez.com
www.oscargimenez.com
**Glasier, Erica**
email: Erica@EricaGlasier.com
www.EricaGlasier.com
**Gonzalez, Juan**
email: juanillustrator@msn.com
www.juangonzalez.co.uk
**Gonzalez, Yolanda**
email: yolanda@yodraws.com
www.yodraws.com
**Green, Alex**
email: algreen@zoom.co.uk
www.alexgreen-illustration.co.uk
**Gross, Sherill**
email: art@sagworks.com
www.sagworks.com
**Gurevich, Leonid**
email: GustavClimt2002@aol.com
www.LeonidGurevich.com

**Hansen, Lærke Melgaard**
email: l.melgaard-hansen@rca.ac.uk

**Hayasaki, Chico**
Represented by CWC International
email: agent@cwc-i.com
www.cwc-i.com
**Hellström, Monica**
Represented by Anna Goodson
Management Inc.
email: info@agoodson.com
www.agoodson.com
**Hollister, Matthew**
email:
matt@keystonecommonwealth.com
www.keystonecommonwealth.com
**Hellovon**
email: say@hellovon.com
www.hellovon.com
**Holman, James**
email: jamesholman1@hotmail.com
**Holmes, Stuart**
email: sh@stuartholmes.com
www.stuartholmes.com
Represented by Illustration Ltd
www.illustrationweb.com/
stuartholmes
**Howells, Tania**
email: tania@taniahowells.com
www.taniahowells.com
**Hughes, Rian**
email address: rian@rianhughes.com
www.rianhughes.com
Represented by Device
email: info@devicefonts.co.uk
www.devicefonts.co.uk

**Iurissevich, Giulio**
email address: iuri.g@aliceposta.it
www.giulio-iurissevich.com

**Jacobs, Irene**
email: info@im-jac.com
www.im-jac.com
**James, Helen**
Represented by New Division
email: info@newdivision.com
www.newdivision.com
**Jamtli, Kaja**
email: kalijam@hotmail.com
**Jaring, Jason V**
email: jasonjaring@gmail.com
ccc.1asphost.com/shiftklick
**Jeffcoat, Anna Olivia**
email: annajeffcoat@hotmail.com
**Jensen-Collman, Nina**
email: ninakjcollman@hotmail.com

**Joaquin, Javier**
Represented by The Organisation
email: info@organisart.co.uk
www.organisart.co.uk

**Jome, Hayato**
email: jome@j.email.ne.jp
www.peacecard.com/jome.html

**Joshi, Varshesh**
email: Varshesh@shoonyadesign.net
www.shoonyadesign.net

**Kawahiro, Yurikov**
Represented by Asterisk Inc.
email: info@pict-web.com
www.pict-web.com

**Kayukawa, Yumiko**
email: Yumiko@SweetYumiko.com
www.SweetYumiko.com

**Kelly, Genevieve**
email:
genevieve@rareandwelldone.com
www.rareandwelldone.com

**Kendall, Kyra**
email: kyrakendall@mac.com
www.kyrakendall.com

**King, Christopher**
email: chris@antiknowsbest.com
Represented by Illustration Ltd
email: team@illustrationweb.com
www.illustrationweb.com/ChrisKing/

**Kiper, Anna**
email: annakip@yahoo.com
www.geocities.com/annakip/

**Kloster, Julian**
email: juliankloster@hotmail.com

**Knight, David**
email: dknight1@uclan.ac.uk
vusi@bamstylee.com
www.bamstylee.com

**Konstantinova, Elena Lavdovskaya**
email: elavdovskaya@tsum.ru

**Kuichi, Tatsuro**
email: me@tatsurokiuchi.com
sally@heflinreps.com
www.tatsurokiuchi.com
www.heflinreps.com

**Lai, Manna**
email: mannalai@gmail.com

**Laine, Laura**
email: laulaine@gmail.com
www.lauralaine.net

**Laita, Monica**
Represented by New Division
email: info@newdivision.com
www.newdivision.com

**Lardot, Christophe**
Represented by Chez Antoine –
Illustration
email: info@chezantoine.com
www.chezantoine.com

**Larrett, Nick**
email: n.l@fashion-
communications.de
www.fashion-communications.de

**Lathbury, Kristie Jarita**
kristie@adamloveseve.com.au
www.adamloveseve.com.au

**Lawlor, Terence**
www.lawlorcollage.com
Represented by Meiklejohn
Illustration
email: info@meiklejohn.co.uk
www.meiklejohn.co.uk

**Lee, Jeeyun**
email: jeeyunlee@earthlink.net
www.jeeyunlee.com

**Lee, Taryn**
email: tarynjlee@hotmail.com
www.coroflot.com/taryn_lee
www.jakandjil.com
www.portfolios.com/taryn

**Li, Domanic**
Represented by The Organisation
email: info@organisart.co.uk
www.organisart.co.uk

**Lomax, Liz**
email: liz@lizlomax.com
www.lizlomax.com

**Long, Xing Jun**
email: matahari.kecil@gmail.com
www.artwanted.com/xingjunlong
coffecat-jun.deviantart.com
www.jotterpro.com

**Longhurst, Kim**
email: kim@ionaccess.co.za

**Lopetz:BD**
www.lopetz.com
Represented by Büro Destruct
email: lopetz@burodestruct.net
www.burodestruct.net

**Losana, Amparo**
email: aplosana@hotmail.com
www.amparolosana.com

**Lui, Janet Pui Kee**
email: netlui@hotmail.com

**Lulu**
email: lulu@plasticpirate.com
www.plasticpirate.com
Represented by CWC International
email: agent@cwc-i.com
www.cwc-i.com

**Lynch, Tiffany**
Represented by New Division
email: info@newdivision.com
www.newdivision.com

**McCafferty, Laura**
email: laura@lauramccafferty.com
www.lauramccafferty.com

**McCaffrey, Christy**
email: cmac1984@earthlink.net
altpick.com/cmccaffrey

**McKenney, J David**
email: jdavidmckenney@gmail.com
www.jdavidmckenney.com

**McMahon, Claire**
email:
claire_e_mcmahon@yahoo.co.uk
www.clairemcmahon.com

**Mackie, Daniel**
email: daniel@danielmackie.co.uk
www.danielmackie.co.uk

**Maclean, Fiona**
email: fiona@fionamaclean.com
www.fionamaclean.com

**MacLeod, Lucy**
email: info@lucymacleod.com
www.lucymacleod.com
Represented by PVUK.com Ltd
www.pvuk.com/news
email: create@pvuk.com

**Maraz, Carlos**
email: cmaraz@marazdesign.com
www.marazdesign.com

**Masa**
email: info@masa.com.ve
www.masa.com.ve

**Mason, Stuart**
email: Stuart14P@aol.com

**Masunouchi, Asako**
email: mail@asako-masunouchi.com
www.asako-masunouchi.com

**Matsubara, Shiho**
Represented by Asterisk Inc.
email: info@pict-web.com
www.pict-web.com

**Matveeva, Ekaterina**
email: info@mambeeba.com
www.mambeeba.com

**Mazo, Ariel**
email: ariel@ademure.com

**Mazzesi, Nicoletta**
email: nmazzesi@nmazzesi.com
www.nmazzesi.com

**Menisha**
Represented by Chez Antoine –
Illustration Management
email: info@chezantoine.com
www.chezantoine.com

**Messenger, Rachel**
email:
messenger_rachel@yahoo.co.uk

**Modén, Kari**
email: kari@moden.se
www.karimoden.se

**Mount, Arthur**
email: arthur@arthurmount.com
www.arthurmount.com

**Mueller, Astrid
(Potatomammadesign)**
email:
info@potatomammadesign.com
www.potatomammadesign.com

**Mulawka, Jeff**
email: jeffmulawka@hotmail.com
www.jeffmulawka.com
www.altpick.com/jeffmulawka

**Murray, Wayne**
Represented by Wayne Snooze
email: wayne@snoozelab.com

**Nagamiya, Yoco**
Represented by Asterisk Inc.
email: info@pict-web.com
www.pict-web.com

**Naro, Michinori**
Represented by Asterisk Inc.
email: info@pict-web.com
www.pict-web.com

**Niles, Laura**
email: laura_niles@hotmail.com
www.myspace.com/lauramichelleniles

**Nwokedi, David**
email: david@insidethecreative.com
www.insidethecreative.com

**O'Hora, Zachariah**
email: zach@zohora.com
www.zohora.com

**O'Malley, Jason**
email: aero68@mac.com
www.jasonomalley.com

O'Neill, Jacquie
email: jacquie@jacquieoneill.com
www.jacquieoneill.com

Obasi, Henry
Studio: PPAINT
email: chenna@ppaint.net
www.ppaint.net
Agent: UNIT
email: chenna@ppaint.net
www.unit.nl

Paull, Jacqui & Carl Melegari
www.jpaullmelegari.com
Represented by PVUK.com Ltd
www.pvuk.com/news
email: create@pvuk.com

Parentela, Claudio
email: c_parentela@libero.it
www.claudioparentela.com

Pariseau, Pierrre-Paul
Represented by The Organisation
email: info@organisart.co.uk
www.organisart.co.uk

Peach, Emily
email: emilypeach80@yahoo.co.uk

Peker, Dilek
Represented by d+design
email: info@dpiudesign.com
www.dpiudesign.com

Peluffo, Marcella
email: marcella.peluffo@fastwebnet.it
www.marcella.peluffo.com

Persson, Stina
www.stinapersson.com
Represented by CWC International
email: agent@cwc-i.com
www.cwc-i.com
Represented in Asia by Cross World
Connections
Tokyo, Japan
www.cwctokyo.com

Pilar, Bella
www.bellapilar.com
Represented by Magnet Reps
email: art@magnetreps.com
www.magnetreps.com

Pinglet
email: pinglet@email.com
www.pinglet.com

Ponce, Diana
email: info@dianaponceart.com
www.dianaponceart.com

Potts, Andy
email: info@andy-potts.com

www.andy-potts.com

Prang, Katherine
email: katprange@yahoo.co.uk
www.myspace.com/prangay

Prikryl, John
email: jprikryl@gmail.com

Pring, Sally
email: mail@sallypring.com
www.sallypring.com

Reece, Gavin
Represented by New Division
email: info@newdivision.com
www.newdivision.com

Renault, Dorothea
Represented by Chez Antoine –
Illustration Management
email: info@chezantoine.com
www.chezantoine.com

Rodriguez, Edel
email: edelrodriguez@aol.com
www.altpick.com/edel

Rosen, Kim
email: kim@kimrosen.com
www.kimrosen.com
Represented by Anna Goodson
Management Inc.
email: info@agoodson.com
www.agoodson.com

Rotzsche, Jens
email: jens@adastragrafx.de
www.adastragrafx.de

Saitoh, Yusuke
Represented by Asterisk Inc.
email: info@pict-web.com
www.pict-web.com

Salek, Janis
email: janissalek@verizon.net

Santry, Karen
email: karensantry@verizon.net
www.fashionartbank.com

Saunders, Anna
email: purple_creature@hotmail.com

Sauvage, Marguerite
email:
contact@margueritesauvage.com
www.margueritesauvage.com

Scandella, Alessandra
email: alefast@fastwebnet.it
www.alessandrascandella.com

Sharp, Erica
email: info@ericasharp.co.uk
www.ericasharp.co.uk

Shaul, Meirav
email: meiravshaul@hotmail.com
www.meiravshaul.com

Shephard, David
Represented by Illustration Ltd
email: team@illustrationweb.com
www.illustrationweb.com

Shimizu, Yuko
email: yuko@yukoart.com
www.yukoart.com

Sibley, Michael
email: mich@elsibley.com
www.msibley.com

Silvestri, Marsha
email: msarts@mindspring.com
www.fashionartbank.com

Smith, Andrew
email:
andysmithdesign@hotmail.co.uk
eldictator.deviantart.com

Smith, Alexander Brooke
email:
alexander@utopiacreative.co.uk
www.utopiacreative.co.uk

Srimekhanond, Prot
email: thisispin@yahoo.com
www.thisispin.com

Stanga, Carlo
email: carlo.stanga@fastwebnet.it
www.carlostanga.com
Represented by Helen Ravenhill
email: hravenhill@earthlink.net

Stolle, Rainer
email: illu@rainerstolle.eu
rainer@brotundbutter.de
www.rainerstolle.eu
www.gotique.de

Storey, Anton
email: antonstorey@mail.nu

Suhariyan, Sonya
email: sonyasuhariyan@gmail.com
www.sonyasuhariyan.com

Symbolon
email: info@symbolon.jp
www.symbolon.jp

Tabib, Lior Yefet
email: liortab@yahoo.com

Tate, Jamal 'Bam'
email: darkreign@mac.com
web.mac.com/darkreign/iWeb/
DARKREIGN/DARKREIGN.html

Teng, LiXan
email: leashapore@gmail.com
leashapore.deviantart.com

Throup, Aitor
email: info@aitorthroup.com
www.aitorthroup.com

Tjader, Ella
Represented by Illustration Ltd
email: team@illustrationweb.com
www.illustrationweb.com/ellatjader/

Townsend, Claire
email:
claire.townsend@hotmail.co.uk

Townsend, Marina A
email:
marina_townsend@yahoo.co.uk
marina.artistportfolio.net
www.artshole.co.uk/marinatownsend.htm

Truman, Lucy
Represented by New Division
email: info@newdivision.com
www.newdivision.com

Tuomaala, Anna
email: annatuomaala@yahoo.com

Turner, Helen
email: turnerpictures@aol.com
www.helen-turner.co.uk

Turner, Sarah
email: sarah.a.turner@hotmail.com

Unger, Tanya
email:
contact@honeybeeillustration.com
www.honeybeeillustration.com

Uriarte, Borja
email: uriouria@hotmail.com

Verhoye, Annabelle J
email: anna@annabelleverhoye.com
www.annabelleverhoye.com

von Huijkelom, Margot Mace
Represented by Agent 002
www.agent002.com

Wacker, Kerstin
email: info@wacker1.com
www.wacker1.com

Wai
email: wai@netspace.net.au
Represented by Illustration Ltd
email: team@illustrationweb.com
www.illustrationweb.com/Wai

Waite, Gemma
email: gemm83@hotmail.co.uk

Malena Gagliesi
Lipstick Personality, Figure
magazine, NYC (2003)
Adobe Illustrator